WOMEN INNOVATORS

VOL. 7

Tamara Patzer

Table of Contents

Meet the Women Innovators

Introduction

The women who contributed their time and energy into the interviews and this book, have amazing stories to tell of how they created success from tragedy, developed tenacity during and after tragedy, and became their own version of success. The Women Innovators series was created as a space for women who needed a place to raise their voices and share their wisdom. This is Volume 7 in the Women Innovators series.

Foreword

The dictionary describes an innovator as "a person who introduces new methods, ideas, or products." My mind conjures up images of pioneers, creators, and brilliant people.

In today's noisy, busy world one would think that there is "nothing new under the sun." However, because the world is so connected, and we are consistently bombarded with the latest of inventions and technology, that we must be creative and innovative to be able to adapt and thrive.

In this book, you will read of women who have done just that. Some have gone to the "bottom of the pit," so to speak, then had the courage to rise above, figure out what was at the root of their upheaval and then find a solution.

All have, at the root of their beingness, the heart to share, and give, becoming a force for change in our world. These women are not content to keep their light "under a bushel basket," but rather share their innovative thinking, ideas, and products for the world to enjoy.

This book is a gift to you, our readers. May it inspire you, spur your innovative spirit to action, and provide a blueprint for living life fully, with contentment and joy. If you are struggling right now, know you are not alone. Know that there is a sisterhood waiting to lock arms and lift you up with support and care.

- Becky Norwood

Debra Crosby

Debra Crosby turns entrepreneurs into sought after speakers, thought leaders and luminaries who command the stage by teaching them how to communicate in a clear, concise, confident and compelling manner. She's passionate about working with speakers who want to deliver messages, solutions and ideas that have the potential to unite us as one, global tribe.

The founder of the Present to Prosper Studio, and creator of the TED Talk Blueprint for Successful Speeches program, she brings to her practice more than 30 years of experience as a professional presenter, trainer and producer. She trains her clients to infuse multimedia and multisensory experiences into their presentations so that they can deepen the learning process and the impact for their audience.

She also helps clients weave spellbinding stories and authentic vulnerability into their talks, so they can connect with, and match the energy of their audience with warmth in a meaningful way. Bottom line: this blue haired goddess of unconditional friendliness shows you how to own the stage and yet how to be playful with your audience at the same time. Debra has taught 1,000s of people how to successfully present themselves via TV, public speaking engagements and in Hollywood films. Her clients have presented at national conferences, booked paid speaking gigs across the US, and landed high-profile media appearances.

Create Your TED Talk Blueprint

Tami Patzer: *I'm really thrilled to have you Debra because, my goodness, everybody's like, "Who is that lady with the blue hair who's always "rocking' it?"* I just love that! The goddess of unconditional friendliness. That is just such a beautiful, beautiful line. And, to look at you and meet you, you really are that person! You emit it, and I love that. *I want to get right into our interview, so of course my big question is: Who do you help?*

Debra Crosby: My special niche is working with authors who may also be coaches, but specifically professionals who have a spiritual platform. My ideal client is intentional about the manner in which they operate in the world. They have a desire to be more aware and more conscious about how they live. My ideal client aspires to be a luminary. They are usually published authors, but that is not required. They speak to transcendent principles or universal truths. They're not interested in professing a specific religion, but invite the listener to live happier, more rewarding lives, a better quality of life, to have healthier relationships and to create more prosperity from a higher vibration. Those are my ideal clients; shakers and movers. People who are on a quest to have a positive effect in the world while inviting their audience to embrace simple truths of wisdom, peace, happiness, prosperity and abundance.

Tami Patzer: Wow, I think I'm one of your ideal clients! But, I listen to you and I'm like, "Wow, that's exactly what I'm hoping to do to change the world." So, I think that people who operate at this higher level, we, and I'll include myself because I really see myself as a messenger's messenger, we seem to have some special needs and maybe we see ourselves as having problems other people don't have. *What would you say are some of the big problems that people who want to get out there and speak to people in an authentic way face?*

This is so cliché, but people are always talking about, "How do I present on the stage without being salesy even though I want them to participate in buying my products?"

Debra Crosby: Well, first of all, to speak to the first part of your question - because it was a multi-level question - is someone has a big dream. I have a big dream to have a positive impact on the world. You feel inspired, you feel enthusiastic, you feel really passionate about that big dream and that big goal. That's the beginning of a hero's journey. This common language that's being used out there as sort of the buzz word, but I got interested in Joseph Campbell way back in the day. So, when the hero, or the heroine, begins on their journey there are inevitably going to be challenges. Now, in mythological language, those challenges would have been dragons, right? Or a big tiger! But honestly, internally, those dragons are metaphors for our own internal resistance. The problem I find, is that folks have this big dream, but their experience will create internal resistance that shows up in like "I can't do this. This is too big. I'm not good enough. I have to do some more preparation. How dare I?" All this stuff comes up, right? So, I have tools in my tool bag as a coach, a certified life coach, to circumvent the internal resistance so that they're liberated. Their energy is liberated. I'll say it this way. Einstein said, "Match the frequency of that which you want to manifest, and it will be so. This is science, this is not philosophy." One of the ways I work with clients, is to release and liberate their energy so their energy is matching the dream and the idea they want to manifest. That is the way I help people. Is that cool, or what? It is a signature process that I call RADICAL FREEDOM.

Tami Patzer: *That is really cool, because I'm listening and that is often something that people will say: "Who am I to do this?" Even Napoleon Hill asked himself that question: "Who am I to tell people what it takes to get rich?" when he was told, "You should spend 20 years working on this project" That was a question he asked, but* *that's really interesting. So, you help people to get out of their own way?*

Debra Crosby: Yes, fundamentally when someone signs up for my TED Talk Blueprint for Successful Speeches program, the first three sessions what I refer to as RADICAL FREEDOM(c) where we work on their energy and work on clearing any internal resistance so that they can manifest what they want. I start energetically first. And then we work on the actual practical, step-by-step approach to writing the content, and then how to figure out what you want to say, why you want to say it, who you want to say it to, what's your motivation, what's your core passion, and then, how to turn that into a performance. Shakespeare said, "All the world's a stage." Well, it really is! It's not just about writing what you need to say, but it's how to deliver what you need to say. That's what I have in the TED Talk Blueprint for Successful Speeches. But fundamentally, at the core, it starts with energy, and having your energy in alignment and in a really clear place.

Tami Patzer: *How long does the TED Talk Blueprint take to accomplish?*

Debra Crosby: Three months. 90 days of process, and it starts out with, you said the first three sessions.

Tami Patzer: *Are these sessions once a week, how does that all work?*

Debra Crosby: Once a week. The majority of my clients I see via video conference, and what's wonderful is it gets recorded, so they get a copy of their training, and they can review that at any point in terms of what we did in that session.

Tami Patzer: *So, a TED Talk is, what, 15 minutes typically of a really impactful presentation? When they're done with that, are they ready to do a TED Talk. Do you have any success stories of people who have done that?*

Debra Crosby: I've transitioned from being an artist/educator for the Wang Center for The Performing Arts in Boston from being a television host on broadcast television to a home audience of 2.5 Million and my career keeps evolving. So, it's a relatively new concept of working with folks who want to be on TED stage, so I'm just finishing this year 2017 working with folks who want to go on the TED stage. I'm really excited that I will have folks on the TED stage, but I already have used that TED Talk Blueprint for Successful Speeches program to get people on other national stages, including SXSW. So, the formula works. The curriculum works. And it's just matter of time before seeing myself and other folks on that TED stage.

Tami Patzer: I think that's really interesting because people, they see the TED talks. And I actually saw, it was Jane Fonda who was talking about the third act, and it really triggered something in me when I saw Jane Fonda talking at a TED talk because I used to do the Jane Fonda exercise. That really dates me! But, I'll tell you, it worked so that was really interesting. *So, tell me more about some of the things you talked a little bit about the limiting beliefs people have. What do you think some of the big misconceptions or issues are with people when they see you, and they're saying, "Ok, she can help me get on the stage."? But yet, they think they're not ready. Do you have a test or something that you can help people?*

Debra Crosby: I have a screening process. And one is I want to make sure that person had their ducks lined up in a row. So, I speak in public a lot, I love that. Frequently that's how I attract clients. I had a situation where someone wanted to meet with me, and I realized at the end of that conversation, they didn't even have a website. They didn't even know how to use social media. There were a lot of things that they didn't have in place, like a structure to be able to move forward. So as a matter of integrity, I said, "I'm going to recommend that you actually work with this entrepreneurial coach, and get all your ducks lined up, and let's talk in about a year when you're ready to get out there."

I want to make sure there's a match, so one of the things that's ideal for me is that someone is either writing a blog, articles, writing a book, or has written a book. That's usually the first thing. And then I also want to know, do they actually have a goal where they have a specific target date where they want to be on stage. Now, it doesn't have to be the TED stage, I just use that formula because I think it's brilliant. It doesn't matter if you want to be a keynote speaker, or if you want to talk on Google talks or you want to talk on UpBound, SXSW, or you've been asked to speak in Las Vegas or even your local Chamber of Commerce.

It does not matter. The TED Talk Blueprint is an excellent blueprint. One of the things I need to know regardless if they are published or not is do they have a motivation and drive? Do they have a target date? Do they have something that they need to be speaking at? Usually they're pretty motivated, in that case.

Tami Patzer: Well, I think that people sometimes do see the vision that's way out there in front of them, but they haven't done all the baby prep things that they need to do. I actually started speaking as a college instructor, then talked a lot at Chamber of Commerce and

Score and SBA. So, most of the speaking that I've done has been as the teacher, and that means that you basically dump all of this information out because they're normally there in a college classroom. They're there to learn about some topic. *How would you say that speaking on the stage is different from teaching in front of a classroom?*

Debra Crosby: Well, that's an excellent question and you and I have a very similar background, or a similar life calling, and I've been a teacher as well. The difference, in terms of speaking on TED is that you have a core story, and in that core story you're presenting is, authentic vulnerability. You're exposing some aspect of yourself in terms of a challenge or a problem or a difficulty, or something that you're trying to improve or overcome.

And you have this one idea that has occurred to you as a result of your own story, then you've done some research. So, your story isn't just subjective, you have substantiated the subjective with objective research, statistics and quantifiable anecdotes. And that's the difference between just teaching and being on the TED stage.

Tamara, I feel that when you're on the TED stage, you are actually a teacher. But, it's a little bit of a different formula because you're not there to lecture at people. That's a real no-no, on TED stage it should feel like a conversation. It should feel like a love affair. It should feel like a real connection and a sharing of ideas that is occurring. So, it is a different paradigm than traditional teaching and lecturing.

Tami Patzer: I really like the way that you described that because, just like our interviews, it's conversation. And I'm hoping that the people are like leaning in to listen (or read). You know if you've ever been in a restaurant and all of a sudden you realized that everyone is listening to your conversation because it's so interesting, and it's things they've never heard about before.

Debra Crosby: Well there's a whole bunch of people leaning in right now!

Tami Patzer: I'm leaning in because I'm really listening. I want to make it clear, "the TED Talk formula" doesn't mean you're only going to speak at a TED Talk. It's a really brilliant formula for speaking in general on any stage.

Debra Crosby: Yes. Do you want to know why? Because you have 15-18 minutes to get your message across! You do not have the luxury of a half hour, 45 minutes or an hour. You have to be clear, you have to be concise and you have to be compelling. You cannot afford extraneous information, so it's this squeeze box where you have got to really focus on what's essential. I love that!

Tami Patzer: Here's a question, and I want to know so I'm sure other people do. *How do you choose the stories you tell? If I'm trying to talk about why you should write a book, for example, to become the authority. How do I choose the stories that make me human, but at the same time move the story forward? Because I tell some things that are extremely personal. Should I choose business related stories, or the fact that I wrote the Girl Scout news when I was in the third grade? So, it's like I had a calling that happened way back then. How do I choose my stories for my 15 minutes?*

Debra Crosby: That is such an excellent question, and I'm going to preface that with, I look forward to seeing you on the TED stage. You are ready! You are ready, and you have so much to say, and that TED stage opens you up to the globe, everybody on the planet, and it gives you the opportunity to connect with people in a really powerful way. So, if you have a book and that book has a message, then we focus on the message of that book. The first question I have is, first answer, what are you most passionate about in the world? Can you articulate that, Tami?

Tami Patzer: What I'm most passionate about right now is I'm really excited about what I call being the messenger's messenger, and helping heart-centered people, conscious people or spiritual people like you. Your description was perfect; get their messages out. Because I have all of this background in media and platforms that I help them create, so that's what I'm really passionate about. It's helping others get their messages out to the masses.

Debra Crosby: So why, at a core level in terms of your core, as the heart of who you are, why is that important? I invite you to just take a second before you just give me the answer. At the heart of who you are, why is that important?

Tami Patzer: I think because when I was little, I always was told that little girls are seen and not heard. I've always been held, I hit that glass ceiling and I think having a voice and being able to say who you are and what is important to you, is really important. So, it's the voice, and breaking that glass ceiling is something important to me because I always had to be 50 billion times better than everyone else, just to get my little 50 cent raise.

Debra Crosby: Wow! See now, I love that! And that would be a title of a TED Talk. how is "Being 50 Billion Times Better gave Me a 50 Cent Raise" Isn't that a cool title?

Tami Patzer: Yes, but that's the truth! I think a lot of people, especially women, or maybe a non-white male, they've experienced that exact same thing, or the fact that I drove up and down the highway 67 thousand miles in one year, so I could get my bachelor's degree.

Debra Crosby: So how did you break that glass ceiling from being that little girl?

Tami Patzer: I just kept showing up and moving forward, and every time I got the opportunity to be on someone else's stage or to be the success story, that was the goal. I wanted be their success story, so I would do whatever it took then I'd say "Hey, I did this. You told me to do this, I'm now a success." Then I'd get on their stage and then as I grew, each mentor, "Oh, you helped me become a success." I wanted to be the success story and I actually have a photograph of me on my very first stage at Main Street Marketing Machine's on Mike Koenig's stage in San Diego. There were about 700 or so people there, and he gave me 15 minutes, and I titled it "I am a success story." and I'm standing there in front of the screen, and I have that beautiful photo. I just realized just the other day that "I am a success story." must be my theme, because that motivates me because it was, "Get on the stage to tell how what this person's telling you to do, works." So, I did. And you have to provide all this evidence, so that was my motivation. It took me, I think, not even 12 months the first time I did it. So, thank you!

Debra Crosby: Now my next question is, what have you learned from having to be a billion times better? What can you teach others, so they don't have to work so hard at being a billion times better to get the raise? What have you learned to make it easier to shed the light on the path for others, so they don't have to work a billion times harder?

Tami Patzer: Well, number one, don't go after a J.O.B - a job. Number two is, start working on your media exposure. Start getting that online presence just like your example about the author, or the people writing the book, where you sent them back and said, "See me in a year." So, I say, let's start building that online presence, let's start getting content, let's get the media exposure. Every little thing you do, let's promote it so that people know you're the big deal, so that you rise up above the other people and become that top one percent. Because most people, for example, they might do a show like this, and "Hey, it was on! Whoopee!" and they're all happy, and then that's it. They don't do anything else with it. Well, I will take the show, I'll write a press release about it, I'll turn it into a book, I'll show it on YouTube, I'll use it over and over and over again. And a month from now, I'll do it all over again to keep it fresh because I know that only a very small percentage of people will see this at any one point in time, so it will always be new to someone, and keep working for us 24/6 365. That's my big vision. That's what I can do for people so that instead of a year, we could do that in 30-90 days and that person could come back to you and say "Ok, I've got my infrastructure. I'm somebody who is now available to do your TED Talk program."

Debra Crosby: So, what I hear you saying, is that you provide the structure and the support, so people can work smarter, not harder.

Tami Patzer: Right! You have worked a bazillion times harder so that the folks you work with can work - smarter, not harder. Right, I can cut years off the learning curve. Years!

Debra Crosby: Yeah! So, don't you think that's important to get that message out there? Isn't there a sense of urgency to be providing solutions to this world right now? And don't we need to start finding solutions faster and faster?

Tami Patzer: *Yes.*

Debra Crosby: You're a shaker, a mover and a thought leader!

Tami Patzer: Thank you! What I really like is, obviously for everyone listening or reading, this is a really good example of how Debra can help you. She just took me and, just to let everyone know, this was not any rehearsed thing. This is a real fly on the wall conversation. *Do you see how Debra took me, used me as an example and pulled out that based on my question well, what could I use as an example?*

Debra Crosby: And of course, I gave her a couple of things that came to mind in this moment and then she said, "Think about that." So how cool is that, that everyone has just witnessed a really good example of how Debra works and her energy? Just to let you know, as I was describing all this, I had what I call those "angel goosebumps" where you know that the truth is rising, and I had that significant energy shift. So again, I'm experiencing with Debra exactly how she works with people. "How cool is that?

Exactly! So, at the foundation of how I operate is unconditional friendliness. I'm listening to you and, I'm your guest, but the way I roll in the world is I'm acting as if we are already friends. And as your friend, you asked me a question, but I knew that the question really had a deeper question in terms of YOU, who you are and what you are about. I just follow my own genuine curiosity. Yes, I have significant training, I am training out the wazoo on how to do that effectively and efficiently. Also, energetically, thoughts have a frequency. So, if I'm asking questions based on genuine curiosity and wonder about who you are and what you're about and what your life purpose is. Your thoughts are going to come from a higher place, and that's going to raise your vibration, so you get what you call "angel boosts" Well, through that process of inquiry, where I am genuinely interested in who you are and what you're about, your frequency is naturally going to rise!

Tami Patzer: That's really phenomenal.

Debra Crosby: Just in that process. I'm really excited for you after this conversation! What's going to happen next in your life? Seriously! I'm not kidding. I have these kinds of conversations with people and all of a sudden, they've been asked to speak at a major conference because their frequency was brought up to a higher level. They started thinking on a higher-level of consciousness.

Tami Patzer: That is interesting because, when you decided to be part of the Women Innovators project, I was like "WOW! How cool is that?" And then of course, here we are today! I was really excited because you have such a phenomenal background, it's like "Whoa!" And Present to Prosper, how beautiful is that? Because, so many people today, they want to learn about how to present to prosper and you have just, again, we demonstrated how you're able to work with someone who has that deep desire to be what I call a messenger, and you helped me to crystalize more of my purpose in just a short conversation.

You also did something that I think everyone loves, and you confirmed to me that I'm on the right path. What a gift that you're giving to me and everyone listening! Because so many people today, they're ready. They're ready to present, and they're ready to prosper. So, I just think that the name of what you do is so beautiful. And of course, the successful speeches program is something that is really phenomenal. *Is there anything else that you'd like to address before*

I ask you where we can find out more information about you and your services?

Debra Crosby: Well, I want to cycle back, in that you asked me originally what story to tell. Now that we know that your skill and your assets and your support, and your calling and purpose in life is to make it possible for folks to work smarter, not harder, because you've already worked a bazillion times harder for them. Then we can cycle back and figure out what story best illustrates that point. So, what learning did you experience where you went "Ah-ha, I don't have to work so hard anymore!" That's how you cycle back through this process, we start asking questions, and then we figure out what story best showcases that message and that idea. I just wanted to go back. So, speaking to Present to Prosper, it's a play on words. When you are fully present in the moment, as Eckhart Tolle says, you're giving the best of yourself to your audience. And that's a gift. Right? When you're present, you are giving a present, to your audience. I chose the word "prosper" over the word "profit" because for me, I speak to audiences that are interested in spiritual principles, are more enlightened, conscious, awake and heart centered individuals. So, the word "prosper" for me, felt more holistic and win-win. It's not just I profit, but we all benefit. The word "prosper" encompasses abundance and wealth. Right!

Opposed to I win, and you lose, which is an old paradigm. It's the "old boys'" network, which talks about "I profit." It's we win, and we all prosper. When we share ideas, and that's what I love about TED Talks, and I'm going to segue into TED Talks. TED Talks is a global platform where we share ideas that make the audience think about themselves, their lives, their relationships and the world in a new and fresh way. And at the end of the TED Talk, people are invited to a call to action to do something about what they learned. Right? And you have only 18 minutes to get that across. That's what I love about TED Talks.

So, Present to Prosper is about how you present your ideas, your message and your story to ignite and galvanize your audience into action, so they can think differently about themselves, their life, the world, in a new and fresh way. And the other thing I love about TED Talks, is it's this platform where all ideas are valued, appreciated and respected. In that environment, we have the potential to become and see ourselves as one global tribe.

The clock is ticking, and we are in a tipping point in terms of where we are at on the planet. If you listen to Jane Goodall's talk on YouTube about where we are right now, she talks about a core truth. We are at a tipping point, and we need to find some solutions, and we need to be thinking together creatively and collaboratively. That's what I love about TED Talks, and that's why I have created a curriculum around TED Talks, because we have got to get our ideas out there.

It doesn't have to be the TED stage, it could be in your local Chamber of Commerce. It can be as a keynote speaker. It can be at any other stage out there in the world right now where you are getting your ideas across, so we can think about solutions that we are facing in this planet right now in this very moment. That's why I do what I do. I want to assist people to speak their truth, to tell their story, to get their message out so they can be change agents, thought leaders and luminaries in making the world a better place. We have a lot of problems, and we need to solve these problems. We need to get our butts in gear!

Tami Patzer: That's the absolute truth and, wow! I'm really pleased that you decided to be part of the Women Innovators program, too. *Where can we find out more about you and your services?*

Debra Crosby: I have one more question. When do see yourself on the TED stage, Tami?

Tami Patzer: *How long does it take?*

Debra Crosby: 30 days! So, can we see you on the TED stage on 2018?

Tami Patzer: 2018 definitely!

Debra Crosby: Let's make a date!

Tami Patzer: Let's make a date. What do you think, February? Could I do it in February?

Debra Crosby: Let's see you on the TED Stage February 2018! What stage?!

Tami Patzer: Well I live in Florida, so that would be the easiest, but I can go anywhere.

Debra Crosby: So, there's TEDx, that's the easiest way. I'm challenging you to submit to finding in Florida where TEDx is close to you. Submit a proposal. And I look forward to seeing you on the TED stage.

Tami Patzer: Debra Crosby, I accept that challenge. February 2018 TEDx in Florida.

Debra Crosby: Woo hoo! Alright, so how do people find me? I'm fully active on Facebook. On Facebook it's Debra Lee Crosby, and it's not difficult to find me because I have blue hair, and I'm from Salem, Massachusetts.

Tami Patzer: Ok. So, Debra Lee Crosby, Salem Massachusetts, find you there. And definitely.

Debra Crosby: You can connect with me on LinkedIn at: https://www.linkedin.com/in/debra-crosby-3651958/. Or Facebook at: https://www.facebook.com/debraleecrosby

Debra Crosby

Debra turns entrepreneurs into sought after speakers, thought leaders and luminaries who command the stage by teaching them how to communicate in a clear, concise, confident and compelling manner. She's passionate about working with speakers who want to deliver messages, solutions and ideas that have the potential to unite us as one, global tribe. The founder of the Present to Prosper Studio, and creator of the TED Talk Blueprint for Successful Speeches program, she brings to her practice more than 30 years of experience as a professional presenter, trainer and producer. She trains her clients to infuse multimedia and multisensory experiences into their presentations so that they can deepen the learning process and the impact for their audience.

She also helps clients weave spellbinding stories and authentic vulnerability into their talks, so they can connect with, and match the energy of their audience with warmth in a meaningful way. Bottom line: this blue haired goddess of unconditional friendliness shows you how to own the stage and yet how to be playful with your audience at the same time. Debra has taught 1,000s of people how to successfully present themselves via TV, public speaking engagements and in Hollywood films. Her clients have presented at national conferences, booked paid speaking gigs across the US, and landed high-profile media appearances.

Contact Debra Crosby:

LinkedIn: https://www.linkedin.com/in/debra-crosby-3651958

Facebook: https://www.facebook.com/debraleecrosby

Email: debracrosby.present2prosper@gmail.com

Dr. C. Nicole Swiner

Dr. C. Nicole Swiner, MD. a wife, mother of two and she lives in North Carolina. She loves taking care of the family, as a whole, from the cradle to the grave. Her interests include Minority Health, Women's Health and Pediatrics. For her undergraduate education, she attended Duke University, and went to medical school at the Medical University of South Carolina in Charleston, South Carolina. She's lived in the triangle since finishing residency at the University of North Carolina and continues teaching medical students and residents as an adjunct assistant professor with the University's Family Medicine Department. While she's not treating patients at Durham Family Medicine, she's speaking in the community, writing, or spending time with her family. Her passion is making medicine plain to her patients so that all people, from all walks of life, can understand how to take better care of themselves and their family.

How to Avoid
The Superwoman Complex

Tami Patzer: You have written some books that really resonated with me, "How to Avoid the Superwoman Complex" and "How to Avoid the Superwoman Complex: Follow-Up Visit" What fascinated me was the subhead, it was "12 Ways to Balance Mind, Body and Spirit." *Can you give me a little bit about your background about how you came from being this family doctor to be a business boss?*

Dr. C. Nicole Swiner: Business boss, yeah. I like that. So, I was kind of thrown into this entire world of business. I didn't grow up, or go to school, thinking I was ever really going to own a business, or start my own entrepreneurial journey. In medical school, you, unfortunately ... Now, it's a little bit different, but about 10 years ago, we didn't get a lot of business training as medical doctors. You learn the medicine, you learn how to, a little bit, deal with the insurance companies, and learn about all of that, but you really don't get business experience. At least, when I was in school, you didn't get it unless you sought it out. Thankfully, I think students nowadays know that more and so some of them are getting their MBAs while getting their MDs or doing business courses while they're getting their medical degree.

That's great, but when I got out of medical school, or residency, I said, "I'm probably going to end up working for a hospital or maybe a nice community practice and do my thing and be happy."

When I started working here in Durham, fresh out of residency, loving my job, loving my patients, having a great time, the hospital that owned us decided that we weren't really making the profit that they wanted us to make, honestly. So, they ended up coming down

29

with the decision that they were going to close our doors after about
... The practice, before I joined, had probably been in business for
about 10, 11 years, and I had been working, at that point, for about
three years. They said, "Okay. We're going to shut down the doors.
We're going to move you all, you'll have a job. We'll move you to
these fancier practices that we have, in these more Metropolitan areas,
and you'll be fine, and your patients will be fine."

We were a little disappointed. We said, "The practice has been here,
we've been seeing our patients for a decade."

We had about 8,000-10,000 patients that we were serving, at the time,
and I said, "What's going to happen to them?"

So, long story short, we decided, "Okay. There are private practices,
they do exist. We know it's hard, but we love our community, and
love our population of patients enough, that we want to learn the
business of medicine. We want to learn how to run a practice
independently and we could do it."

It was four of us, at the time, who decided to get together and do it.
Thankfully, we're eight years running strong. It's been a journey, we
have hired some good business-minded folk, like a management
company, and my husband who had started his own business by the
time we met, before we even got married. So, who knew how
important his knowledge would be, for me, as a private practice
owner when we got married? We learned as we went, and we finally
feel like, "Okay, we know how to do this."

So, that was kind of the first start of my entrepreneurial journey.

Tami Patzer: I think it's important that people understand, like you said, not everybody gets trained in business. *You were trained to be a doctor-and at this point you found yourself having to make a decision, right? Like, "Do I want to work for somebody else and go do what they tell me to do?" Or, do I want to take this step of faith and serve the people I've grown to love in my own community?*

Dr. C. Nicole Swiner: So, you're absolutely right, it was absolutely a step-out on faith. It was lots of prayer involved, like, "What are we going to do? Who's going to pay the bills? Who's going to pick the insurances for the staff? Who's going to do that?"

I think it was just the right time for things. Sometimes when you're not ready, God is ready, and he just thrusts you into it and He gives you the right people, gives you the right answers that you need at the time. So, it was scary, but we learned a lot, we have learned a lot and we're still learning at this point, and doing pretty well, which is great.

So, then I think once you have an experience like that in your career, in business, after getting over that hump and realizing, "Okay. We didn't sink, we're swimming," I think it makes you less fearful to do other things. So, while we were doing this thing with the private practice, and trying to reestablish ourselves, and rebrand, I said, "Okay. Well, I'm going to get out here, I'm going to go meet some folks, do some church fairs and networking, and all of that."

While I was doing that, I met the editor of a local paper here, called the Triangle Tribute, and shook her hand and was introducing myself. I said, "You know what? I kind of like to write a little bit. I did some journaling when I was younger to kind of keep a diary and all that. I would love to maybe do some medical writing for the community if you have a need for that?"

She said, "Sure."

I didn't know that that point, but that started my book writing desires, and career. With blogging, and with writing, for that paper every couple of weeks, I learned that I like to write in my voice. I write the way that I speak to patients. I try to speak plain English, in terms of medicine, so people can understand. I was getting good feedback online and became familiar with social media. I didn't really like Facebook, or anything like that, at the beginning, but my husband said, "Okay. You're a business owner now. You have to get out there and market, it's free, why not?" Now I'm addicted. So, it was his fault.

Tami Patzer: I think you said the magic word, which was fear. Many people, they never think about that, but local newspapers, local radio, local publications, they're always looking for expert advisors. And often they will say, "Write up 500 or 1000 words and send it in." I was an editor and had lots of conversations like you did. *How many articles did you write before it became clear to you, "Hey! I think I have a book?"*

Dr. C. Nicole Swiner: It was years. I did not have a book in mind, probably five to six years in. I was happy getting a little bit of ... They gave me a couple of dollars for gas money to write the articles and I thought that was cool. People were recognizing my name in the community and inviting me to come to their functions and events to do small speaking things. So, I was content, but once I became more familiar with social media, I joined some organizations, or some groups, on social media. You have to do that. In business, you have to join interest groups. That's how we met, Tami. We met by being part of the same interest group on Facebook, but after seeing that and seeing other medical colleagues around me publishing books and other people, in general, particularly people that were self-publishing, I said, "Hm. That's interesting. How can I reuse all of this stuff?"

I had been writing, at least, once or twice per month, for years. So I said, "Well, how can I reuse this? How can I spread this word? How can I broaden my reach?" I said, "I'm going to write a book!"

Literally one day I woke up and a light bulb went off, that's how it was. It took years. I didn't think about it until years later.

Tami Patzer: A lot of people don't realize they already have the content for a book because they have been participating in, either social media, or even way back in the day when it was typewritten they were still creating media. Believe me, I used to get handwritten articles that I would have to type in and edit, but today everything is digital. People write on their Facebook posts, they write on LinkedIn, or maybe they have a blog. So, you are, I guess, an example of someone who stepped back. It sounds like your husband helped you a lot. You stepped back, and you saw a bigger possibility. In Content Marketing, content online is King, and if you are someone who writes a lot, you probably have a book or two in there. *Can you tell us a little more about your books that you've written in your themes?*

Dr. C. Nicole Swiner: So, once I decided, "Okay. I'll write a book. Let's see how that works," I went back and looked at some of the blogs, and some of the articles that I had previously posted, and a lot of them already had the theme of minority in women's health. While all this was going on, my husband and I got married, we were starting a family, the private practice was starting. So, all of these transitions were happening in my personal life. So, I kind of combined the things that I had already written about different elements of health ... The first book has a lot of so-called, random, topics; Allergies and high blood pressure and chronic cough. Things you wouldn't even really attribute, or associate, with the Superwoman Complex, but all of them have to do with mind, body and spirit, as a whole.

So, I took those things that I wrote from a medical perspective and combined them with some things that I had learned either on my own personal journey, becoming a mom ... At the point of the first book I'd had my first child and was pregnant with my second child. So, going through some of the stressors, going through some of the, "How do we do it all," and then talking to patients who ... A large majority of my patients are either young women, or young families, and seeing them going through some similar things with stressors and ending up coming to me talking about their stress, their depression, their insomnia, their chronic pain, or headaches and realizing, "You know what? I think a lot of this is a common theme with the majority of women. We're trying to do it all. We're trying to be Superwoman."

I said, "Aha! Let's write about that. Let's include that because as a family doc, I can associate almost any disease, any medical condition, any mental health condition to stress, to trying to do it all, to be a Superwoman, or Superman."

It was interesting how my life, and my journey, paralleled that of many of my patients. We may deal with things in an unusual way, or cope with things in a different way, but we're all dealing with a little bit of that same underlying stress of just trying to manage everyone, and everything, in our lives and then at the end of the day, often neglecting ourselves. So, that's what the Superwoman complex is about and that's what I like to talk about.

Tami Patzer: I know at one point in my life, I actually counted all of the things I needed to do, and I came up with like 23. I needed to be

23 people, to be a mom, to do the house cleaning, to go to work, I was going to school; I was like the ultimate juggler and it led me to get sick— I actually ended up with stomach problems. I think about the Superwoman Complex, and like you said, even the Superman Complex, but we're focusing on women because women seem to feel this pressure to do everything. It's a sense of responsibility that weighs heavy, especially when you have children. It's like, you will put yourself on the back burner because you are focusing on making sure that those children have everything they need and you're hoping that you're doing the right thing, so they grow up to be good people. That leads to all kinds of things. ***In your follow-up visit book, what did you expand on in the second book?***

Dr. C. Nicole Swiner: So, the second book is going to print as we speak, it will be out in the next month or so, but the first book, "How to Avoid the Superwoman Complex," which is available on Amazon by the way. We'll talk about that later. It breaks down a lot of different what you would even consider random medical things, but then ties it all in together with the Superwoman, the theme of women trying to take care of everyone, do everything, and medical issues that can either be associated with, or caused by the Superwoman Complex.

The follow-up visit is more of a handbook on, "Okay. We know we have it, it exists, now what are we going to do about it?"

So, since the first book came out, I've been doing some speaking, and some teaching, and doing things at conferences about it. But I've gotten a little bit clearer about, "Okay. So, I've learned some lessons along the way about how to make life a little bit easier, how to take better care of yourself, how to be more self-aware. So, now I'm going to share these secrets a little bit in more detail."

So, now it's a little more focused on, "Okay. We now know what the Superwoman Complex means, we know the signs and symptoms, but now here are some ways to truly make life easier for yourself."

Tami Patzer: *Can you give us, maybe, just a little taste of one, or two, examples of what you can do to help yourself?* I actually saw one of your t-shirts with the big, "No! No Superwoman!" slogan.

Dr. C. Nicole Swiner: My big three are pretty consistent in both books. My number one is sleep, that's one of my favorite topics to talk about. Actually, it's the first chapter in the first book, it's called Sweet Sleep. Get rest. Get rest. So many of us ... There's this cute meme I saw, literally, within the last day or so that said, "There's a such thing as, I think a mom zombie, or a mombie". The definition is, a mom who is super exhausted, but still stays up all night 'cause it's the only kid free time she gets. Go to sleep. Don't be a mombie, or a mom zombie, go to sleep because you have to rejuvenate yourself. You have to let your mind and your body rest or there are dire consequences. So, some way, somehow, figure out how to get better rest. I go into detail a lot in the book about the problems that can cause insomnia, or reasons why you might have insomnia and ways to fix it. That's always number one.

Number two is, ask for help. A lot of Superwomen, or Power Women, as we were talking about earlier before the broadcast, we often feel like not only can we do it all, but we feel guilty for asking for help. Or we feel that it's a sign of weakness, or that it will be used against us if we ask anyone to help. And that's just not true. There are very rare cases where there are evil people in your circle that will expect something from you, or use it against you later if you ask them, if they're going to the store, pick something up that you need really quick. Or become part of a drop-off team so that you can share picking up and dropping off your kids to certain activities. Or, if you need someone to come vacuum really quick. I have wonderful employees at my practice that are young, and don't have kids, and want a little bit of extra gas money. They love to come and tidy up my playroom, or babysit. Ask for little pieces of breaks that you can just sit and breathe.

You mentioned the 23 things on your list. It's almost impossible to get those things done without feeling burnt out. So, ask people to help. Ask the hubs to cook a couple of times a week so that gives you a little bit of a break. It's okay.

My last, and my favorite, which is probably the most difficult one is, to learn to say no. How powerful is that? Do you say no well?

Tami Patzer: I have put myself in overwhelm and I get what you're saying, "Go get rest," and "Don't stay up all night trying to work." Learning how to say "no" is difficult. I think I sleep well, but I probably don't ask for help as much as I should. I think the third one, "saying no" is the hardest. I was thinking, "Oh my goodness she caught me," because that is one of the hardest things that we have to do because there's just so much happening.

I want to go back and talk more about your success as a blogger, social media person, and a writer, and maybe ask you for some tips about how anyone can use these tools because your husband said it, "Hey! It's free!"

As we know, there are free things, and then there are things that free equals time, but it doesn't take cash out of your pocket. *Can you give some of our readers tips about how you developed into who you are today, you have a thriving medical practice, and also, a publishing business.*

Dr. C. Nicole Swiner: I understand everyone's situation is different, but I'm blessed to have control over my schedule. If you work for someone you may not be able to do that as easily. Definitely look at your schedule and see where you might be able to carve out some time for those special interests. Or if you're starting a new business that you want to develop, but you still need to work that main job as your bread and butter, which I completely understand, until hopefully that side gig becomes your main gig, carve out some time as much as you can. So, if you can ask for a half day, a day off, or administrative time, or first thing Saturday morning before the kids get up, you get up and carve out that time. Carve out some time to do it because as you said, it's free, but it does take time and effort. Once you get it going and get your routine going with social media, and know when to post, and how to post, it does become quite easy.

So, what I did, overtime, was the book came out, excuse me, once I was speaking, once I was doing some broadcasting on Periscope and all that, what my hope, at some point, is to do medicine part-time. For now, I take Friday's off. Like today, while I'm here at home, I can do Doc Swiner stuff, but if there's a way that you can maybe cut back a little bit or carve out some specific time for your special interests so that you can plan your posts, you can do live broadcasting, or do a Podcast, like Ms. Tami is doing. Make it a priority. So, you say, "Okay. I'm going to really try to do this. I want to get 1,000 followers by whatever month. So, I'm really-"I'm really going to get serious about this as a business."

So, that's one. Number two, you don't have to be overwhelmed by doing all of these things at one time. There are a million and one, seemingly, ways to be on social media. Whether it's on Facebook or

Instagram, using Skype, Periscoping. I would say pick your favorite three, and I think I looked at a Forbes list recently that said, "The big three are Facebook, Instagram and Twitter."

If you pick those three, and become proficient in those three, then that's a great start. I would say at least post once daily, if not, more than once. Once you get your feet wet, post once, at least daily, on each of those three, to really broaden your reach.

The third little tip that I like to tell people about is, there are these websites and systems that you can become a member of. You can do it for free or you can purchase their program, where you can manage all of your social media from one place. I don't know, Ms. Tami, do you do Hootsuite, or any of the other types of social media control systems?

Tami Patzer: I have used Hootsuite. I've also tried Post Planner. There are really good ones like BuzzFeed. I also found that I could educate myself in the car while driving by either listening to Podcasts or informational CDs. Like you said, using these automation tools is important. The big thing about automation, of course, is to choose one that works for you, and find some time. When I first started, I actually worked full-time, and it took me six months before I was able to go full-time doing what I do, which is social media marketing. That's what I started out doing back in 2009. Our guest today did just that, she consumed content, took time to create and then she did the ultimate thing: She wrote a book. *Can you tell us a little bit about how writing a book change your life?*

Dr. C. Nicole Swiner: So, you know, there are some of us who are lucky enough to have a huge publishing company to come and give you a million dollars to write a book. But there are most of us, who end up self-publishing, and using your book for different purposes. So, I think the book has been a major help in my blossoming speaking career. So, now I'm doing the speaking thing, and I want to do that seriously and professionally, so that it can ... Like I said, my goal is to be able to do medicine part-time and do this more than part-time because now it's become a passion.

My book has served as my business card, it's served as my resume, it gets my foot in the door a little bit easier. I was at a pretty good presence as a doc in the community, but now I'm a doc and an author, and people see you more as an expert on that topic. So, I think it's tremendous, especially if you're trying to switch careers, if you want to do speaking and do a lot of those things professionally, you almost have to have a book nowadays to get your foot in the door.

Tami Patzer: It makes a huge difference. *Do you have any speaking engagements coming up?*

Dr. C. Nicole Swiner: I'm traveling to Oklahoma City in August. It's with a friend of mine named Wyjuana Montgomery, who's another Duke grad, and she has a phenomenal organization for women, and young women, named Reach Forward. She does a No Fear Women's Conference every year, and I'm blessed to be returning. This will be my second time presenting there and that is in August. I'm very excited about that. If you go to my Doc Swiner Facebook Page, I have the date, and the flyer, and all that. If you happen to in the area, that'd be great.

Tami Patzer: *Where can people find out more about you?*

Dr. C. Nicole Swiner: I am easily findable on Doc Swiner. Here's my website it is http://www.docswiner.com On Facebook, I try to use DocSwiner almost everywhere to be consistent. That's another social media tip, by the way, let me throw that out. So, whenever you figure out how to be on social media, try to be consistent so people know how to find you easily. So, that was a freebie. So, docswiner.com is my main website. On Facebook, Instagram, Twitter, I'm DocSwiner. I have the book available on my website, I also have it available through Amazon and we've launched our No Superwoman Store, which is an easy place to get the books. You can pre-order the second book. The Follow-Up Visit is coming out this Summer. It's http://bit.ly/thedocswinersstore.

Tami Patzer: You intrigued me with your t-shirts. ***Tell me a little bit about the Doc Swiner product line that you came up with.*** That is an entrepreneurial idea. Not only is she a speaker, an author, fearless entrepreneur, but she's also created branding for her books and her t-shirts. That's a million-dollar idea right there.

Dr. C. Nicole Swiner: Again, I blame my husband, who is a marketing genius. So, he has his own graphic web design, photo and production company called Spider Marketing. He, about a year ago, launched a t-shirt portion of that company. So, I watched him, literally behind me here in the basement, he has equipment to press t-shirts, and he has designed them, and printed, and all that stuff. So, while I was making the book I said, "Hmm." I would come downstairs and watch him. I said, "I want to make the t-shirt too. That would be cool."

Then, again, from meeting people, from networking, from seeing my colleagues, other folks who had written books, when you go to conferences, and go to events, and you want to sell your book, it's nice to also have something else to sell just in case, maybe, they don't want to read a book, but they'll rock your t-shirt. They'll represent for you with your t-shirt.

So, the first t-shirt that came out, and you'll see it on the sight, is the No Superwoman. So, it's a symbol, the circle with the slash for No, and Superwoman on it. That was the first idea for branding. Then, as I decided I wanted to turn this into a career, and do speaking, and all that, we branded it so that it was more generic Doc Swiner. So, that's when the Doc Swiner tee came out. It has my favorite saying on the back that we came up with. It said, "You don't have to be Superwoman in order to be a Super Woman."

So, don't stress yourself out all the time. So, that's where those two ideas came out. The most recent thing I came up with was a Superwoman sleep serum. Did you see that, Tami?

Tami Patzer: No, I didn't. I just saw the Superwoman and I saw your photo and thought, "Wow she really knows who she is!"

Dr. C. Nicole Swiner: Like opening up your shirt, coming out. My assistant has her own side gig where she makes organic hand, body, and facial products from home. So, she mixes 'em up and puts natural ingredients in them. I treat a lot of patients, as I mentioned, with insomnia, and sleep issues, and hormonal issues. I said, "Amy, you're making these body creams, and these wonderful emollients for the face and the body."

I said, "What if we came up with our own sleep recipe? So, you have your stuff where you put shea butter, coconut oil, lavender, and all that, but there are natural things that can help sleep like lavender, and like Melatonin, for instance, evening primrose oil, if you've heard of these things. You can get these things naturally, form the store, and they occur naturally in the body and can act like hormones, and sleep hormones."

I said, "What if we found those organically, put 'em into a liquid, put 'em into a lotion, or cream, and people can use it on their body? Brilliant!"

She went on-line, purchased the organic products, made it in her kitchen, and that's what we've been giving and selling now. It's called Superwoman Sleep Serum, and I will say, we've gotten rave reviews about how it feels good on the skin. You put it on head to toe and it helps you to rest better. We've been really pleased. So, that's the newest thing on the on-line store. I'm really excited about that.

Tami Patzer: I think our big message today, and it goes back into every single thing that you've said ... You've talked about how you started out in the medical profession, not ever thinking about being an entrepreneur, but yet you found that you needed to become an entrepreneur. You stepped out in faith, and even though there was fear to step out, you did it anyway. It's kind of like, "Woah," and you flew and took simple steps to improve your life.

I think that everyone listening should really go take a look at Doc Swiner's website and you'll see that, despite the anti-Superwoman, she does have, again, this power that exudes. You'll see it in the imaging, and when you read her books, I think you'll really get that sense of where she's coming from and everything. I'm very interested in staying on top of your Superwoman Series. *I have a feeling that book number one, book number two, that there's going to be a book number three that is going to continue on this theme, and help people with their journeys', as they understand that you don't have to be a Superwoman if you use DocSwiner's advice. Get rest, ask for help, and just say no.*

Dr. C. Nicole Swiner

C. Nicole Swiner, MD. a wife, mother of two and she lives in North Carolina. She loves taking care of the family, as a whole, from the cradle to the grave. Her interests include Minority Health, Women's Health and Pediatrics. For her undergraduate education, she attended Duke University, and went to medical school at the Medical University of South Carolina in Charleston, South Carolina. She's lived in the triangle since finishing residency at the University of North Carolina, and continues teaching medical students and residents as an adjunct assistant professor with the University's Family Medicine Department. While she's not treating patients at Durham Family Medicine, she's speaking in the community, writing, or spending time with her family. Her passion is making medicine plain to her patients so that all people, from all walks of life, can understand how to take better care of themselves and their family.

Contact Dr. C. Nicole Swiner, MD

Website: http://bit.ly/thedocswinersstore

Email: info@docswiner.com

Twitter: http://www.twitter.com/docswiner

Dr. Heather Tucker

Heather Tucker is a Life Harmony Coach, speaker, and trainer. She teaches women entrepreneurs how to strengthen their relationships with themselves and others. Her areas of expertise include communication mastery, emotional intelligence, technology harmony, and energy work for strengthening the mind, body and spirit connection. She guides her clients and students to have more harmony in their personal and professional lives, lead their companies with more momentum, develop more peace of mind with technology, and increase their online presence. Dr. Tucker has more than 12 years of higher education teaching and research experience, as well as a natural gift for easily working with others.

Dr. Tucker has a PhD of Human-Computer Interaction, as well as a Bachelor of Science in Computer Science. Prior to co-founding her company, Another Level Living, LLC, Dr. Tucker held the position of Assistant Academic Program Manager for the Department of

Information Technology at Mt. Washington College, as well as Intelligent Technologies Researcher for the Army Research Laboratory. Dr. Tucker's work has been published in many journals, conference proceedings, and books.

Creating More Harmony
in Your Relationships

Tami Patzer: Your background is really fascinating. I actually thought about doing work in human-computer interaction, because I really think that that is a really pertinent topic today about how we interact with our computers, and how it's literally changing us and the way our brains work, and everything. But before I take up the whole conversation with my thrill at talking to you, tell me more about what you're doing now, and who you help.

Dr. Heather Tucker: Right now, I am working with a lot of women entrepreneurs. I have men who also come as students, as well. So, I work 1-on-1 with women entrepreneurs who want to have more harmony in their professional and personal lives. I also am teaching classes for people who want to also become a coach, or learn what coaches is about. So, I have clients, and I also have students. I have been teaching for so many years for the universities, and now I'm teaching for a company, and it's just been so wonderful.

You're right about technology, and how it has changed everything. It was really exciting that I actually took the time to study that and learn that. This has been a progression since shortly before 2000; paying attention the evolution, and paying attention to how our interaction with technology has changed over time paying so close attention to it, and becoming more aware of what's happening. A lot of times my clients come to because they are overwhelmed with technology.

Dr. Heather Tucker: They don't necessarily know how to deal with it. They try to figure out what technology should they use, or what should they be doing in order to take their company to the next level.

Working with me has been causing a lot of big shifts, especially in their understanding of how to align their passion, their purpose and their profits. Strengthening that communication with themselves has helped them to be able expand their vision for the future, as well as live 100% present in the now.

And that's by healing the past. That's really what we focus on; healing the past, letting go of a lot of things that hold us back, our negative emotions of anger, sadness, fear, hurt, and guilt. Or even our limiting beliefs, we may believe that we're not good enough, and "Who are we do this?" All these things are just things we've decided a long time ago. And the reality, what I tell my clients and students is, that whoever you think you are, you're so much more than that.

Let's tap into that full potential power, so therefore you can be who you are meant to be, do what you're meant to do and have the things you're meant to have, with ease.

Tami Patzer: You know, it's really funny, as I'm listening to you. Just last night, I had a mentor tell me, "Tami, you need to be more human! You need to focus less on business! You need to be in the now." And you just said that, so I'm sitting here going, "Hmm. Two days in a row, same message. Pay attention." So, tell me more about, in the work that you do with people, when they come to you, what are two or three examples of what their biggest struggles and issues are that you can help solve.

Dr. Heather Tucker: We have so many different areas of life, and we tend to focus on the areas of life that we're good at, like our careers. We tend to neglect some of those areas that we're not necessarily good at, like our families and our relationships. A lot of times, the more we ignore or avoid the areas that we don't want to pay attention to, the more those areas come and try to show examples in our life where we want to keep going, but we reach a block.

A lot of times, my clients come to me after a significant emotional event, like the loss of a loved one, them having marriage difficulties, or having health issues. The Number 1 thing that derails us can be our physical health. So, we look at health as total health, including spiritual, emotional and physical health. We end up strengthening those. And then, we look at not only the health for that individual, but the health in their life, in all of those areas of life. Have you ever been so overwhelmed that you feel like all areas of your life are on red alert?

Tami Patzer: Yes! Sometimes, it can be a trigger. It can be something simple. For example, I went to the grocery store, and I wanted a raspberry turnover. Not peach, not apple, and they didn't have it. It was like, "Hey!" I was disappointed to the point that I actually talked to the person stocking for like 5 minutes about, "Why in the world would they not stock raspberry turnovers?!" In the world, obviously, raspberry turnovers are not a big deal.

Dr. Heather Tucker: But then, if you look at everything in context, sometimes you just have a bad day where it seems like no matter what you do, it doesn't go right. And people will say, "You're attracting this energy!" And you may be, but sometimes I think we do get overwhelmed, especially because of technology. What I discovered about technology is the expectation for you to create and deliver in the snap of a finger, when people used to expect things to take weeks or even months to create.

Tami Patzer: Now people think, "Oh, you can do this in 24 hours, you can do this in 5 minutes." I find that very stressful, and it does go into my personal life. And when you said that about, "We like to do the things we're good at and avoid the things we're not." Yeah, I'm pretty good at business, but I'm not very good at personal relationships, other than I can be a good mother. But I'm not good at having romantic relationships. So, I can see that I'm off balance.

Dr. Heather Tucker: Yeah, well you know what? The beautiful thing is - and this is what I teach my clients - we celebrate those overreactions, and we celebrate those imbalances. I tell them that this is where we are. Cool. Now, how do we bridge the gap from where we are to where we want to be? It's so interesting that you told me about this story about the raspberry turnover. Because a lot of times, we overreact. I had a big overreaction of a situation that happened at Best Buy, and then when it came down to it, I realized it had nothing to do with that situation.

I really had to look deeper and figure out what was causing it, and a lot of times, when I have my clients celebrate their overreactions, we're able to really be able to figure out what the root cause of that problem is and take care of it. Then, it's no longer an issue. So, the biggest piece is really our mental and emotional part, which a lot of times, is what causes us to overwhelm with technology. Actually, kids are even more overwhelmed with technology than we are. That's one of the things. There have been studies that have talked about this, and that's why we're losing that human element, because we do want things NOW. We do want things better, faster and cheaper.

Dr. Heather Tucker: Right now, I'm in Hawaii - Aloha! - and I've been here for the last two weeks. And one of the things that's so unique about their culture that we have kind of forgotten is that, if we just be, then things will take care of themselves. A lot of times, we end up doing and having things, but we don't know how to just be. Just to be in that moment. And we create that busyness in our lives.

Sometimes when we're too busy, we miss something. A lot of times, even parents struggle with trying to figure out what that connection is with their kids, or even trying to figure out what's their connection with their parents.

The beautiful thing about working with me, we help take care of all of that with ease, because it all starts with our mindset. Really, it starts from above in terms of spiritual, bringing that energy down. But when the energy comes down or an idea or thought comes down, it's usually our mindset of, "I can't do this," or our feelings; "Oh, this is too difficult to handle." that prevent us from really being able to manifest the things that we want in our life.

And one other thing I tell my clients, that we talk about all the time is that life is too short not to enjoy it. Not to be happy. Not to be healthy. Not to be prosperous. And the body, the physical body, it can heal itself. And I teach my clients how to be their own doctor first. How to decrease their blood pressure with ease. How to get rid of their diabetes. How to change anything that's going on with their body easily.

The reason why we have a lot of health issues is because of a lot of the mental and emotional turmoil and stress that we put on ourselves. It all gets manifested in our physical body.

Tami Patzer: I really believe that, because I'm a perfect example. I ended up having my gallbladder removed because I had golf ball-sized gallstone, and it was causing issues, it was so big. And I know that was created from stress from a previous job I was in where I was just under constant stress. Even my eyesight improved when I quit working in a bad job situation. My eyesight improved! All of a sudden, I could see. I think you're right on target. You're in Hawaii right now for a very important conference or training. Can you tell me a little bit more about that?

Dr. Heather Tucker: Oh, yes. Absolutely. One of the things that makes what we do so great is, we incorporate energy. It's all about energy; everything is all about energy. The energy that we have, the energy that we see. The training that I'm here for is called "Huna." It's an ancient Hawaiian system of energy. The Hawaiians believe that when you're connected to the land, and when you take care of the land, the land takes care of you.

It's like the opposite of what it is here on the mainland. When you can connect to the elements like the earth, the air, the water and the fire, and they resonate with you, it allows you to be able to tap into more of who you are. It's one of the things we use, we incorporate this type of energy in my practice. It's what makes helping people release those negative emotions so easily. Just one session with me can bring clarity to any problem with ease, because it's all about energy. We learn how to be able to pull down energy and be a conduit. The energy does not come through me, a lot of people think, "Wow, Heather, you're so powerful!" It has nothing to do with me.

There's three things that I require for everyone I work with.

1. Their permission
2. Knowing that I'm just a conduit and a guide,
3. And that the energy comes from a greater source above.

I look at it like the Holy Spirit when it comes into you and through you, and how you're able to help push that out to other people. Now, it's interesting that you mentioned eyesight. That's one of the things, when you release negative emotions. I wear glasses myself, Tami, now my eyesight is actually getting even better. Because, there was a time in my life where it's like, I made a decision that I didn't want to see, and that's what made my eyesight worse. But by going back, to be able to give myself permission to see clearly again... It's amazing how I can see. There's actually a book that's called, "Take Off Your Glasses and See" or something like that. Which I have not read yet, but I look forward to it because it talks about this very thing.

Tami Patzer: Oh, that's interesting. Well, that was one of the things I noticed, because I literally could not see. Let's say that if I was at a grocery store and would look up at the words to see what was in that aisle, and it would be blurry. And then after I got out of the bad job situation, I'm going, "Whoa, I can read! I can see signs, I can see distance, I can see in front of me." A lot of people talk about the fact that they have to wear reading glasses, and I don't wear reading glasses at all. And I'm probably 20 years after most people start wearing reading glasses.

So, you're there learning this ancient Hawaiian energy healing, and I actually experienced it. And I have to say that during the time, I was like, "Is it working? I don't know." But, the next day I definitely did feel and have the realization that I had a clearing of some ancient history that dates back to when I was about 20 years old. That was a really phenomenal thing, so that was why I was so excited about talking to you. So, when you work with people, do you work with them long distance - like ours, obviously, Hawaii to Florida - so obviously you can work with people all over the world. How do you typically do that, over the phone, Skype? How do you do that?

Dr. Heather Tucker: Usually, we do it via Zoom, or we'll do video conferencing. Not Skype, I use Zoom, and also, I will do it over the phone. As a matter of fact, shortly after we worked, I had did it over Skype with someone in Saudi Arabia. So, it works anywhere.

Typically, I like to do face-to-face, so therefore there's that connection. But we don't necessarily have to do that, it can also be over the phone as well.

One of the things, the whole reason a lot of people ask me why would I go from IT, something it was easy, no problem making 6-figures in, to starting my own business and starting from scratch. Well, the answer is: my own health was failing. And with all of these techniques, I've been able to restore my health so well that I'm looking forward to helping other people too.

Tami Patzer: Oh wow, that's really cool. *So, can you give me some ways for people to make contact with you?*

Dr. Heather Tucker: Please check out our website, AnotherLevelLiving.com. We are also on Facebook and Twitter. We have not only a business page for Another Level Living, I also have my own Facebook and Twitter page; Dr. Heather Tucker. So, look me up and follow me on there. I'll be talking about different stuff that's not necessarily under the company. And we also will be on YouTube. We're definitely looking forward to being more well-known. Books are coming out as well, so looking forward to hearing from everyone out there.

Tami Patzer: So, you have some forthcoming books, and you also do speaking as well as the group or one-on-one training, so you actually do go and speak to large groups and travel around the country doing that. I really am fascinated by your background because, again, that human-computer interaction, that doctorate, I can imagine that we could probably have a whole interview on just what that's all about. And then, of course, how you're merging the energy with that, as well as the life harmony.

I think that's the keyword, and that's the vibe that you send to send off, to me, is balance and harmony. That's the feeling I get, and I remember in your introduction, it was saying you have a natural gift to be able to work with others. And I think that's the energy I get from you, even though we're I don't even know how many, 10,000 miles apart right now. That is the energy that you emit through the atmosphere is one of balance and harmony.

Dr. Heather Tucker: Life harmony. That's what it's all about. Just by calling myself that when I first got to it, the Universe was like, "OK, let's prove it." And it's all about how, regardless of what comes to you, it doesn't matter what comes to you, it's "How do you respond?" And "What does it mean?" And then, "How do we utilize what happened in an easy, positive way to move forward?" So, I'm all about that life harmony and balance.

Dr. Heather Tucker

Heather Tucker is a Life Harmony Coach, speaker, and trainer. She teaches women entrepreneurs how to strengthen their relationships with themselves and others. Her areas of expertise include communication mastery, emotional intelligence, technology harmony, and energy work for strengthening the mind, body and spirit connection. She guides her clients and students to have more harmony in their personal and professional lives, lead their companies with more momentum, develop more peace of mind with technology, and increase their online presence. Dr. Tucker has more than 12 years of higher education teaching and research experience, as well as a natural gift for easily working with others.

Contact Dr. Heather Tucker:

Website: http://www.AnotherLevelLiving.com

Facebook: http://www.facebook.com/AnotherLevelLiving

WOMEN INNOVATORS

Twitter: http://www.twitter.com/AnotherLevelLiving

Becky Norwood

Becky Norwood is an International Bestselling Author, Speaker, and Coach. She also assists her clients to publish their books. She has brought over 35 authors to #1 bestseller in many different genres, including children's books. Leading by example, knowing how our stories can impact the world, her book, "The Woman I Love: Surviving, Healing and Thriving after a childhood of Sexual, Emotional and Physical Abuse," has laid the groundwork for her coaching programs. Her ongoing book interview series, the second of which will publish in late February 2018, "We Choose to Thrive: Our Voices Rise in Unison to Spread a Message of Inspiration and Hope for Abuse Survivors has had over 50 participants, courageous women sharing their stories.

Choosing to Thrive After Extreme Abuse

Tami Patzer: I'm really happy to have you here because I've known you a few years, and most of it has been in an online environment. I have watched you grow, as many of us struggled to find your way in the sea of internet marketing and to establish our online authority. *Tell me more about who you help, and how you got here today.* I'm going to let you tell your story, so don't expect me to say too many things until when I'm curious.

Becky Norwood: I'm so happy to be here. As you said, we met several years ago, learning how to do internet marketing. We both were helping our local businesses, clients, to understand all the nuances of getting their businesses online. The economy was a mess about the time we and there were numerous constant changes within the internet industry.

We both have done well in this field. And we both also added book publishing into the mix so that our clients could use their books to establish their expertise.

On a personal level though, I had a deep underlying issue that kept me from living a truly happy life, and it kept resurfacing. There was always an undertow of depression that hung like a cloud, and I had to give a lot of thought to that.

At one of the training events we both attended on about book publishing, they spoke of the value of leaving a legacy. As I contemplated the message, I knew it was time to make a change for myself. I decided I would write my story. At that moment, I came up with the title of my book, "The Woman I Love." Because of the depth of emotion in the story, it took me five long years to follow through and write it.

My deeply personal story was one that I hesitated to share with the world until finally, at another book publishing event a dear friend of mine challenged me by asking, "Why haven't you told your story?"

Finally, I knew it was time. It took me about three months. I wrote and cried. Mine is a story of sexual, emotional, physical, and mental abuse that started as a very young child. What I did not know was that I was not alone in this devastating experience. It is estimated that one out of three women and one out of five women have had some variation of this type of abuse. I published my story on my 60th birthday, and it resulted in my being able to write a new story for myself. It helped me to understand my worth, and the value what I offer the world. After publishing, I was both shocked and blessed at how many people reached out to me, thanking me for sharing my story and what an impact it had on them. It was a transformational time in my life, and still is!

Since that time, while my main source of revenue comes from the authors I work with, I have also created coaching programs. I have met many women and men who have gone through the same experience. Discovering for the first time in my life what an epidemic this is in our world let me understand the importance of speaking up and telling my story. This epidemic has created a world with a lot of people broken.

So many of us who have gone through this experience in life, are truly good people but don't know how to rise above it. We feel alone, ashamed, and less than, even though we work hard to live a life that is "normal."

My coaching program is called, "The Healing Power of Story." I work with individuals to help them realize what they do want for their life and help them learn to speak up, to stand up, to claim their inner power and know their truth. This has been an amazing process.

In February of 2018, I am publishing the second of a series of books called "We Choose to Thrive." Every chapter features another woman telling her story. They are from every walk of life, from every background. It is so touching and amazing. Over fifty women have participated so far.

Tami Patzer: Wow! So by telling your story, it took you five years to gain the courage to write it. *What were you afraid would happen if you told your story?*

Becky Norwood: We live in such shame, and we blame ourselves. I had no idea that others went through this because I kept my mouth shut. You don't speak about this. There are fear and shame, and we are faced with the impact of speaking up.

Sitting down and writing my story brought up so much I had tried to erase. And, we try to block it out, and for many of us, we can't remember the full details until we do start writing. For me, the depression that felt like a wet, heavy blanket, and that I had constantly battled for so many years, dissipated after I wrote my story. In fact, now, it seldom visits me.

Although I cried through the writing of my story, it changed me. That is not to say that something will trigger from time to time. But I have learned to catch it and nip it in the bud, whether I start singing or do something funny. When I notice a bout of depression coming on, due to something triggering me, I've learned that I can just change the effects and longevity of it immensely. The writing of it did indeed create a new story for me. It transformed my life. And, I see that in my clients now.

Tami Patzer: *When you work with women, and men too with your new author and coaching program are you helping them tell their story, write their story? Is that what your coaching program is all about?*

Becky Norwood: It involves writing, and we start with small exercises because we are sometimes we are resistant to writing it. We start with journaling and writing what little things we remember. I always start my courses with mindset. I feel like the mindset for all of us is such an important factor. I ask questions like what do you want more of in your life. What's happening in your life that's not serving you. Getting down deep what would make you feel alive and more vibrant. What are you grateful for? I ask questions like what good qualities have come to you as a result of your experience. Because sometimes we can't find anything to be grateful for or see anything good. My courses are not short-term because it's something that takes time to put these stories together. Not everyone will publish because a lot of times there is family still alive and it's not safe. But the writing of the story whether they share it with the world or not still starts a new story. I have some that are sitting on their story waiting, and others who may never write their stories. I have some that have written their stories and have published. I do not write their stories. They do, and the results are amazing.

There are more and more women realizing that it's time to speak up, give it a voice because of the impact it's had on our world. We want to be part of the change and create awareness. The biggest awareness is writing the story.

Tami Patzer: *So, you are talking about the biggest reason for people to even explore writing their own story, what makes it so important that you share your story with other people beyond yourself, or is this important?*

Becky Norwood: For many people, it is important because we want to send a message that we can get better, that we can heal. Every person is different. I have found for me to tell the world, not only did I expose it, it let it free. I am to the point in this life that I don't have most of those family members still living. My mom is alive. She read the book and hated it at first, but now she has begun healing. It has made an impact on her life. She realizes the role she played because she didn't stand up. For my family, it has brought healing, and for the most part, the transformation that it bought for myself, is the same freedom I see happening for people that finally get that voice and find their voice. If they don't choose to tell the whole world, at least facing the issues themselves, and, perhaps sharing with their families, brings the healing they need.

Tami Patzer: I think you are right that it starts with you. Often, we are so busy taking care of other people, as you said, we will forget things. That is our protection, and then, of course, I know even in my own business, I know that if I write things down it will be a lot better, for whatever reason I don't know. It's a protective thing because we know the act of writing is revealing. As you said, you spent a lot of time crying, and I guess processing a childhood experience. Like you said your mother, she didn't like the book, but she learned from it because she was part of the experience in some way. I find that's very interesting about how some people maybe they don't share it with other people or the world because they have family members they are protecting. ***So, in the process of coaching people now, how long do people typically work with you?***

Becky Norwood: Typically, it's an 18-month program. This is something that doesn't happen overnight. It's processing. There are ups and downs along the way. The whole thing about it is honoring where we have come from, the gaining of that strength. My motto is, "make the rest of your years the best of your years." It doesn't matter the age. I have young women; one is in my "We Choose to Thrive" book just turned 30 and is a single mom. It was her grandfather that had molested her for many years during her childhood. There were many others he had molested. Her case was the only one that stood because of the statute of limitations. He only received a sentence of three years and served only 18 months. But what it did for her to stand for herself has made all the difference in her world. You know, when you understand the statistics and long-range effects on the person, we owe it to ourselves, and to our family and to the world to heal from it. We need to heal from it because it affects every aspect of our lives. It affects our business, it affects our family, because there are always those trigger points. If we are not able to get over those things it impacts how we treat our family and react to things in business in life. It is time to transform our world, one person at a time.

Tami Patzer: *So, that transformation, it's a transformation of your soul because you had a damaging event in your life. If you were to suggest to someone, maybe they are not ready for coaching or a group coaching program, what type of tips would you recommend to people just to get started if they are trying to figure out what their story is?*

Becky Norwood: Journaling is a good way to start. If you just write down a smell, what the weather was like, what you were wearing, it starts to flow. Journaling is very positive. There are amazing books out there written on these subjects. I found a book called, "The Courage to Heal." Written over twenty years ago, I find it amazing I didn't know that books like that even existed!

If it is better for you, perhaps start your journey with writing what kind of life you would like to have. Start writing and journaling about your dreams and aspiration for the life you would like to have. How you are reacting to different things and contemplate why you are reacting that way. For some, writing is not going to work.

Some have to take an art or dance class that lets you get that expression out. There's a lot of different healing modalities and writing is not the only one. I have women in my book that use art as their medium and others are using dance, or physical activity, even equine therapy. Find which medium allows you to free yourself.

Tami Patzer: I think that's interesting because as you were talking, I was thinking Art, Writing Speaking, Poetry, and even animals. Some people may volunteer at a shelter. There are a lot of ways to express, you know, you. Writing is always a great way to release because it's such a personal expression. But, dancing or art, I can see that. I always like to paint butterflies, because they are colorful and whimsical, and I think that is why the coloring book craze is so popular.

Becky Norwood: One of my dear friends in Canada does body casts of women from their neck down to their hips and then, the client colors it and puts designs on it to tell their story. I am not sure the process of how she does it, but she's gotten awards all over Canada for this. She has created coloring books of her body casts. They name their body cast and tell a story with it.

I have another girl in my local area who speaks all over the place. Her healing is with animals. She speaks of domestic violence and abuse. She works with animals in the shelter, and those animals have taught her lessons on loving herself. The message here is that there is no one right way. Find what works for you. Do what you need to do to discover what works for you. Writing is certainly not the end all be all. Being coached is not the ultimate cure. My goal is to help people get that ball rolling, to discover what WILL work for them.

Tami Patzer: Anytime you take that step forward with courage, again as you said, you don't want to think about what has happened to you whether it's rape, abuse, incest or even an accident. There's a lot of different traumas that we experience in our lives. *What do you think is the biggest thing holding back from moving forward in this healing process? For example, you said you just turned 60, so this means you lived with this your entire adult life. What was stopping you from healing?*

Becky Norwood: The feeling that you are all alone, and shame. I have an image that I use on social media. It's a young girl wearing sunglasses. On one lens, it says, "The shame they know," and on the other lens it says, "The shame they cannot see." Shame is huge. Fear of what other's think of you is another. Many of us can manage to put up a good exterior around us. Often, no one knows what we suffer from behind closed doors. So, fear and shame. Oftentimes it boils down to those two issues at the core.

Not knowing there is help available to us, we put a wall around ourselves to protect ourselves. As I have healed, I have observed many go through their healing processes. However, not all whom I have met are willing or ready to acknowledge that there is a problem, or for that matter, where that problem originated. I find it curious, and often wonder, "Why are they doing that?" For instance, people begging for money on the streets. I wonder how they got here. There's this brokenness that often comes from something very deep-seated that happened to them. We can rise above it, blossom, and live amazing lives, but we have to do the work that it takes. It starts with loving ourselves enough to do that.

Tami Patzer: So, love yourself, then you can take the step forward. What would you suggest then, I want to take it back to the publishing aspect of it, that's the venue you created. *What steps should someone take to publish that story? Obviously, that's what you do with your book series. Do you want to talk about how that might look?*

Becky Norwood: Yes. I am a firm believer that as you walk through this process if you want to make it be something that you want to put out to the world, and you want to stand on your story, and not in your story, as you start writing, seek support. There are going to be times when it is going to be emotional. Love yourself through the process.

For some, I encourage them to start a Facebook because when it does get time for publishing, and if you want to make an impact, you're going to want to get this message out to the world, you are going to need to have the framework setup. Often, I will have them start their own Facebook group and just start talking about what's in their book. The Facebook group for their book will be named the name of their book. Simply implementing social media to share positive quotes can make a difference. Becoming active on a social media platform helps them establish them establish an online footprint. If seriously interested in making an impact, I encourage them to use video to tell their story.

One of the things that we find is that as they start to tell their story, their courage grows. As they begin to realize the impact of their message, it increases their feelings of worthiness. Some get into public speaking to spread their message. Their story is available to be read by the hearts who want to read it, and by standing in their truth, fearlessly sharing that truth, more hearts are reached.

I do focus on the marketing aspect of the process. Anyone can publish a book, but it will not have the impact if you don't include marketing. Self-publishing is now the thing, and if we don't understand how to get our message out to the world, marketing is the key. I have a course called Beyond Authorship – Your Book is YOUR Business and teaches the fundamentals of marketing.

Tami Patzer: So, you take someone from the idea, or "I am going to tell my story," all the way through the marketing aspects. I call it the "Now What?" After you've written and published your book, the "Now What?" is so important that your book will reach the right people. *You talked about the million-women message movement, and I want to ask you to talk just a little about this message. What exactly and how will that work?*

Becky Norwood: We are still in the planning stages, but I have met so many women who have spoken up and told their stories. I have met many women and one who has just lost her daughter to a drug addiction. She has an amazing story. The title of her book is,

"Still standing after all the Tears." She will be one of the speakers on this tour. We will be going from city to city, and she will be one of our speakers. We don't have all of the sponsors. We will have a group of women with varied messages that will not all be on abuse, sexual abuse or abuse period.

There are some women who, for whatever reasons they have emotional things they deal with constantly dealing. Often the ramifications of abuse are health issues. The message is, you CAN heal. Does it take effort? Yes. Does it take tenacity and dedication? Yes. But it is so worth it! And that is our message.

Tami Patzer: I like that. I am looking forward to hearing more about that. *Where can we find out more about you, repeat your upcoming book projects, what you are working on, and where can we find out more about you?*

Becky Norwood: My website is: http://www.thewomanilove.com. My Facebook is: https://www.facebook.com/thewomanilove1/ And, my email is becky@thewomanIlove.com.

The name of the book coming out is "We Choose to Thrive: Our Voices Rising in Unison to share our Message of Inspiration and Hope for Abuse Survivors."

Tami Patzer: *How many co-authors have participated in your book series?*

Becky Norwood: The first book in this series had thirty women. The second book has twenty women so far. If any of your readers want to participate in telling their stories for the We Choose to Thrive series; they can go to http://thewomanilove.com/invite

Tami Patzer: Wow that's amazing. Again, everyone, Becky Norwood, International Bestselling Author Speaker and Coaching. She has written a book "The Woman I Love – Surviving Healing and Thriving after a Childhood of Sexual, Physical, and Emotional Abuse. We have just talked about her programs and upcoming projects. I am really happy to know you decided to share your story. I appreciate that.

Becky Norwood

Becky Norwood is an International Bestselling Author, Speaker and Coach. She also assists her clients to publish their books. Her own book "The Woman I Love: Surviving, Healing and Thriving after a childhood of Sexual, Emotional and Physical Abuse", has laid the ground work for her coaching programs and her upcoming book interview series, the first of which will publish in late January, "We Choose to Thrive: Our Voices Rise in Unison to Spread a Message of Inspiration and Hope for Abuse Survivors.

Contact Becky Norwood:

Website: http://www.thewomanilove.com

Facebook: https://www.facebook.com/thewomanilove1/

Email: becky@thewomanIlove.com.

Donya Zimmerman

Donya Zimmerman is the principal owner of Powerful Biz Woman. She is a business consultant, mediator, author, show host and public speaker trainer! Donya received her Juris Doctorate (JD) in law from the University of Baltimore Law School. Donya has a weekly segment entitled Powerful Biz Tip of the Week on the radio show Evolutionary Woman hosted by Kahdija Ali that runs every Monday from 5:30 PM to 6:30 PM. She has created the CYA, Cover Your Assets, business training series, which airs every Wednesday and Thursday from 7:30 to 9:30 PM.

The show features guests who educate entrepreneurs on the importance of protecting their assents while in business. Donya has conducted several workshops and speaking engagements on business startups and female entrepreneurship.

The Powerful Business Woman Today

Tami Patzer: *First of all, tell me a little bit more about who is the Powerful Biz Woman?*

Donya Zimmerman: Well, it took me about four years to come up with this business brand, the Powerful Biz Woman, and it took me, because I had a law practice and I had to close it due to mismanagement, finances and client's cases and I had to come up with a way to use what God had given me. The gifts and talents and education He had given me to educate others on the importance of making sure that their business is properly set up and it took me four years to realize who my ideal customer is!

I had to do a lot of soul searching, a lot of research and I realized that there were a lot of women who were in my age group, 35 to 65 years old, who were in the second phase of their life. Either they retired from a job or they were forced out of a job that they had been on for at least 10, 15, 20 years. They got tired of working a 9 to 5 job, they wanted to start their own business, or they wanted to go back to school but, due to family obligations, due to having taken care of everybody else, they didn't take care of themselves.

So basically, the Powerful Biz Woman is a woman between 35 to 65 years old who has finally realized that, in order to take care of others, you have to take care of yourself first. Sometimes you have to put your needs above others in order to be the person that they need you to be.

And a lot of time, that's women, especially in the middle age group, they call us inbetweeners where you still have adult kids at home and you have your parents that you have to take care of and you're, like, busy taking care of everybody else but not yourself. So, what happens is that your mental, physical and spiritual health is affected.

So, the Powerful Biz Woman is someone who know when to take time for herself, knows when she cannot help others, she has to ask for help and is someone who has always dreamed of being an entrepreneur, a business owner and who has finally decided to dust off those dreams of entrepreneurship, and make them a reality of being a full-time entrepreneur and a full-time business owner.

Tami Patzer: Wow, four years for you to come up with Powerful Biz Woman, that you just described people like me! People who have spent their entire life being the caretaker of either small children or other people in their family or even people who, because of the fast-moving pace of technology, we've had to reinvent ourselves over and over and over again to keep up so that we can keep moving forward.

Tell me, you actually wrote about being disbarred and making this major come back in the book collaboration "From Fear to Freedom". Number 1, think about that. You were disbarred so you had to actually step back and admit this to the world. You're actually telling people, "Hey, I went down the lowest point but now I'm on my way back up all the stronger and more powerful for it!" *Tell me, what inspired you to share such a personal, personal story?*

Donya Zimmerman: I have realized that in order for me to fall forward, I had to let go of the guilt and pain of being disbarred as an attorney. I had to realize that my mess could be a powerful message for somebody. I had to turn that mess, that embarrassment into a powerful message to make sure that someone else doesn't go through what I went through, to let people know that no mater what happens in life, you can make it. And it took me meeting with my coach, Laurie Polsa.

I met her at Seventy-Two Hours of Power and she gave me the title disbarred, making a major comeback. I had never shared that story, I would duck and dodge it. I would say, "Oh, I got rid of my law practice because I was tired of the rat race." I was trying to cover up this guilt but once I released it to her, and we sat for a whole half an hour talking, I released it to her, we connected. Because I met her on Facebook, she was going through a lot of stuff.

She was a real estate broker and she had to give up her real estate, her and her husband lost everything in 2008 when, you know, the housing market crashed and, for her to share that story, I said, "Hey, I have a mess that I need to turn into a powerful message and share with the world." So, that's when I decided, when she gave me that title, Tamara, it took me only a day to write that story and once I wrote that story, I released all of that guilt, all of that heavy burden that was laying down my spirit and since then, my creative juices have been flowing.

Since I wrote that book and released it in October of this year, God has opened many, many doors for me. God has made me say, "See, once you let go of that baggage, you make room for greatness and prosperity." But when you hold on to baggage, when you hold on to the guilt trip and all of that, you don't have enough room for God to grow you as a person. But once you release all of that baggage, God can grow you and you just grow and you just become the person that God intended you to be.

Tami Patzer: Wow, that is so powerful, Donya. As you're speaking, I have goosebumps. So, you have been making massive, huge steps forward. You actually have created CYA, I just love that. CYA, Cover Your Assets, business training series and I actually think that's how we may have met at some point is I think you invited me to be a guest on your show and we still have not done that yet, so we will do that, I hope, in the future, but at that time, I started to show up and listen to some of your shows and everyone was like, "Wow, this woman really knows her stuff!" And then you have these phenomenal guests who would share, you know, more phenomenal stuff. *So, tell me more about your radio show, CYA business training series.*

Donya Zimmerman: Well, Tamara, we actually me earlier than that because you had asked me to be a guest on your show and I was telling you about my radio concept and after we did that show, you kinda gave me a free consultation and told me what I needed to do.

See, you give so much away, you don't realize how much you're giving away! And you guided me into creating the CYA, Cover Your Assets, business training series. That's why I tell people, "When you are in this journey, you are not in this journey alone." You find your mentors and you find your business coaches like Tamara, Laurie Polsa, Cheryl Wood, Lisa Nickels, Wayne Murray, Abigail, Natalie Forest, you find those people because there are a lot of people out there who are willing to share with you and whatever you receive from someone, make sure you pass it on. Pay it forward and pass it on to someone else because the blessings that God gives you is intended to put you in a position where you can be a blessing to someone and Tammy is one of those people. If you are looking to start a radio show, if you are looking to do a TV show, she is the best coach to have.

But to get back to CYA, because of you, that's how I came up with CYA, Cover Your Assets, business training series because I had to introduce the Powerful Biz Woman, my business and personal brand

and my products brand to people. I had to let people know who the Powerful Biz Woman was, what services she provided and that's how I used the CYA business training series show as a platform to introduce myself to the world. And then, when I did the CYA business training series, that's when I came up with the Powerful Biz Chatline on Facebook. But I had to watch other people do it before I did it and now, I see the importance.

When people see you on a regular basis opening up your heart, sharing your knowledge with them, they are more willing to go with you on this journey, on this ride. And when I did my Powerful Biz Chat live today, I got two new clients who are willing to go on this journey with me to become full time business owners, full time entrepreneurs. And I had to look at people like you, Tamara, to see how you do it strategically and to see how to do it smartly.

And, to me, you got to have a plan because I wrote out my marketing plan ... I have a business plan but that's one thing I think is important. Always start out with a plan. Write you a ten-page business plan for your business and then write a five-page marketing plan on how to promote, grow that business and let people know and that's how the Powerful Biz Chat and the CYA radio cast came about. Because I sat down and wrote out a plan, I watched people who did it, like yourself and other people and I took a little from this person, took a little from you so that I could create my own and that's what you have to do, you have to be the student first before you can be the master.

Tami Patzer: You know, you're absolutely right about writing out your business plan and your marketing plan because the reality is, you're always marketing, no matter what you're doing, you're always marketing. I'm really happy to hear that you're using the Facebook Live platform for your business. And, you just said it, why would you do that? Because you said, I just got two new clients because they see that you are live, they can see you're authentic and they can tell that you are streaming this out of your soul, this information that you're providing. It's not like you're reading a script, you're there, it's real!

You know, everybody talks about being authentic and transparent but when you're on live, people really can tell who you are, they can hear your voice, they can see your hand movements, they can get all of that, the visual clues and everything that are very helpful. *What else are you working on at this time, Donya?*

Donya Zimmerman: Well, of course I got the book, From Fear to Freedom, Disbarred and Making a Major Comeback, I have one more event that is coming up and it's the Uncuffed Women's Colloquium in Baltimore, Maryland at the Baltimore Marriott Waterfront and I will be a speaker and I will be talking about how to, you know, cover your assets while in business. I'll be giving eight simple tips on how to make sure that you don't lose your shirt while in business.

So that's my last event for 2016 and I'll tell you, 2016 has been amazing! Since 2015, I can say that I finally come into who I am, who the Powerful Biz Woman, CYA, Cover Your Assets, and I had the pleasure of meeting a young lady, Alena Lopez Thomas. She's Grown Woman and I'm Powerful Biz Woman and we provide the same service but she's up north in Boston and I'm down here in South in Maryland.

We decided to partner up, pool our resources together and create the ultimate biz virtual bootcamp and under this umbrella, we have created three virtual summits that will prepare you for business startup.

One, you got to create your great mindset. So that's one of the virtual summits, where we prepare you for being in the mindset of an entrepreneur and not a nine to fiver. And then two, we created a virtual summit where we teach you how to get your finances in order to be ready to open your business.

And then three, we created a eight week boot camp, Virtual Summit Bootcamp, where once you have your mindset, your finances together, we will make sure that your business will be up and running in no more than six months and then our part of the series is that whoever goes to any of our trainings, they get to attend our two day boot camp where, in these two days, we give you all the tools and resources you need to go from aspiring entrepreneur and business owner to a legitimate business owner with a strong financial and legal foundation so that your assets will be covered.

And I am so excited about that! I have a couple of speaking engagements coming up. I mean, I'll be in San Diego, California in May, I'll be in Trenton, New Jersey, no, Newark, New Jersey in June, I will be in Boston, Massachusetts for my own conference, the two-day boot camp and, Tamara, I didn't know I would have my own conference this fast cause I was like, "Oh, I'll do it come September 2017 or 2018." But I said, "No, you going to do it by June." And then I have a couple of speaking engagements that I will be doing in North Carolina and Atlanta, I'll be in Atlanta in July so 2017 is really going to be super amazing. It's going to be 2015 and 2016 triple, double, quadruple. I'm just so looking forward to next year. My 46th birthday is coming up on December the thirtieth, so I'll be 35 on December the thirtieth.

Tami Patzer: Well, happy birthday! You know what, Donya, all of these speaking engagements. *Can you talk a little bit about how you got so many speaking engagements?*

Donya Zimmerman: Well, the thing is, for me, the one thing I have learned, you have to find that platform to market your business. Pick one social media platform as your main platform to market your business. And my main platform is Facebook. That's where the number one women are. If you are a business that is geared to middle aged women between 35 and 80 years old because they are saying that 80 now is middle aged because people are living way past 80. You have to be on Facebook. It's so sad that they said that the middle-aged mothers and grandmothers have chased their children off of Facebook and I believe that to be true. Mostly everybody I see on Facebook are women, middle aged women, between 35 to 80. That's who's on there so you have to find that platform that fits you and I have found all my speaking engagements on Facebook. I'm always looking.

It's one wonderful group and I think your part of it too, Tamara, called the Women's Spear Association and they always have a day, I think it's Tuesdays or Wednesdays, where, if you're looking for speakers for your event, no matter if it's a parkette, your radio show, TV show or your live event, I find a lot of speaking engagements that way. And you got to let people know what you're doing. I hate to advertise a lot. What I realized is I'm advertising every day and you kind of have to mix it up. You got to do live videos, do parkettes, be guests on people's radio shows, and have your promotional flyers together. You got to mix it up and that's how I've gotten these speaking engagements. And also, create your own speaking engagements as well, don't wait for people to provide you platforms. Provide your own platforms.

Tami Patzer: Well, that's what I do is, like, if I can't go then I create my own and you're absolutely right.

Donya Zimmerman: Number one, be prepared. Number two, go seek out groups where they put out calls for speakers and then apply and get on radio shows, get on online shows, go out in your local area and do live events. You have to sometimes go beyond your home town.

Tami Patzer: She said she's going to be out in San Diego, she's going to Boston, she's going to New Jersey, I mean, my goodness gracious, Donya is on fire. *So, we are coming up on the holiday Christmas season, what does this time of year really mean to you, Donya?*

Donya Zimmerman: For me, this time of year means spending quality time with your family. I don't believe in New Year's resolutions. You should always be working on yourself every day to improve yourself. You should always wake up every morning with a blessed heart and I don't do that all the time. Sometimes I wake up grumpy and I have to read my bible. You should have a strong spiritual base. I don't care if you're Muslim, if you're Christian, believe in Buddha, have some form of spiritual base where you spend quality time with God on your own before you start your day because your attitude that you create in the morning with create your aptitude for the rest of the day.

And sometimes, I've had to learn if I wake up grumpy, my day is going to be grumpy. Like this morning, I woke up with a positive attitude, I put my Christmas music on, I was just happy this afternoon. I didn't rush out of bed, I said, "What I'm rushing out of bed for? I don't have nothing to do. Everything that I'm doing is going to be in the evening time." So, I took my time, I chilled, I read my word, I listened to Christmas music, I danced in my room, I got myself energized to come downstairs. You don't have to ... Mix your days up! You don't have to do the same old one dang thing and to me, that's why I love being unemployable and unemployable means that you are entrepreneur and you create your day, how your day will go.

And you don't worry about what other people say and when you're doing this entrepreneurship thing, you should not be afraid because people going to look at you like you're crazy, people going to say, "What is she doing? She's not making money. She's not doing this." They don't see the back story so for me, around Christmas time, between thanksgiving and January 22 is the best time to stop putting in work in your business. So, after all the holidays season, Christmas season is over with, you can reach your ideal customers.

Because since November the 4th, my creative juices have been just flowing. I've been putting out work, I've been doing things, God gives me ideas and I go for it and that's how I been able to reach my ideal customers because while people are still shopping and doing what they have to do, they want a special gift for themselves. Whether it's personal development, professional development or starting their business. So, this is the best time to give out your gifts, to give out your Christmas season offers to people, especially if you're a product, if you provide service, if you're a service business. This is the best time to give out your free offers, is during this time because people may not buy right now but they're going to remember everything you tell them, and they'll be back to you when tax season come, when they done paid off all of their Christmas debt.

Tami Patzer: Well, Donya Zimmerman, you are a true Powerful Biz Woman. I thank you so much for sharing that with us. *Can you give us where we can find out more about you and your services?*

Donya Zimmerman: Well, my email address is dzimmerman36@gmail.com, my phone number is 443-635-4557, again 443-635-4557 but the best place to get me is on Twitter and Facebook. My Twitter handle is FACMBC and just hit me up on Facebook, Donya Zimmerman or just go to my business Facebook page, Powerful Biz Woman. And Facebook is the best place to hit me up because Tamara I tell you, we're always one Facebook. That's our social media platform.

Tami Patzer: Well that is true because, like Donya said, it is where the women aged 35 to 80 years old hang out and these are women who are business women, they're entrepreneurial women and they are very active so wonderful, wonderful insight today, Donya.

Donya Zimmerman: Thank you Tamara for being a great mentor and a great coach and your willingness to share everything you have and if you really, really want to do the PR for your business, start a radio TV show, Tamara Patzer is the best person to get in contact with. I call her the public relations coach. That's what I give her and I'm telling you, I recommend her to everybody I know because she knows her stuff and because of her, this is why I am as far as I am in promoting and growing my business and Tami, I want to thank you so much for everything you have done for me and my career.

Donya Zimmerman

Donya Zimmerman is the principal owner of Powerful Biz Woman. She is a business consultant, mediator, author, show host and public speaker trainer! Donya received her Juris Doctorate (JD) in law from the University of Baltimore Law School. Donya has a weekly segment entitled Powerful Biz Tip of the Week on the radio show Evolutionary Woman hosted by Kahdija Ali that runs every Monday from 5:30 PM to 6:30 PM. She has created the CYA, Cover Your Assets, business training series, which airs every Wednesday and Thursday from 7:30 to 9:30 PM.

The show features guests who educate entrepreneurs on the importance of protecting their assents while in business. Donya has conducted several workshops and speaking engagements on business startups and female entrepreneurship.

Contact Donya Zimmerman:

Website: http://powerfulbizwoman.weebly.com/

Facebook: https://www.facebook.com/PowerfulBizWoman/

WOMEN INNOVATORS

Email: dzimmerman36@gmail.com

Marcella Romoser-Scherer

Marcella Scherer is an expert in her industry with more than 30 years' experience transforming the lives of others from head to toe and inside and out. As a certified image consultant, she empowers women to upscale their image to create a powerful presence that creates powerful results. Marcella's gift is seeing the beauty in others and working with them to alien their outer image with their true and authentic self. She helps leaders to stand in confidence at any stage in their lives.

Power Up Your Wardrobe

Tami Patzer: Marcella has styled countless clients, including professional speakers, authors, leaders, national celebrity and TV personalities to feel confident commanding the stage, boardroom or TV interview with their presence. Alongside her image consulting business, Marcella has built a team of, listens to this, more than 5000 reps and has touched thousands of clients during her 28 years with BeautiControl, a mobile spa, anti-aging, skincare and cosmetics company.

She understands women's needs for taking "Me time", feeling beautiful at all ages, and wanting to look and feel their best in a simplistic way. Marcella works her magic with clients one-on-one, in small groups and in workshops to help women customize their look using color analysis, makeup and skincare, body profiling, personal shopping and wardrobing services. She is also a leadership coach and corporate trainer for business big and small.

She is a sought-after speaker and best-selling author, and her work has been featured on NBC News, Channel 12, ESPN, Kiplinger Report and The Palm Beach Post. Marcella is passionate about being in nature, yoga, skiing, dancing and healthy delicious eating. She lives to travel and explore new places all over the world with her husband Mark. They are celebrating 25 year this year and they've been married for more than 24 years.

I was at a Women's Prosperity Network "The Business of Speaking" event, and Marcella spoke about having an image and having a presence to speak from the stage. In the presentation, I learned so much that the next time people saw me, they said, "Tami, what have you done?" And you know what I had done? I had taken Marcella's advice when I went shopping, and I picked out a few key pieces of clothing in my colors, and BOOM! I suddenly had a more professional, put-together look. So, Marcella, thank you so much for that!

Marcella Romoser-Scherer: Oh, I am so proud of you for taking the information and applying it. The best part is getting the compliments. Don't we love that? It's just, that's what it's all about, right? We show up in a new way that people start to take notice!

Tami Patzer: The compliments are really nice because it tells you that when you learn something and apply it, people really do notice. That's why I think it's important that we learn more about what you do. *You are a certified image consultant, so tell me more about what you do and who you help?*

Marcella Romoser-Scherer: Well, I am all about empowering women from the inside out, and I specifically love to work with entrepreneurs, speakers, coaches, authors, c-suite executives because they're image is really critical to their success. I have a seven-step system that I use, "Upscale Your Image" and the number one thing is: understand the magnitude of your platform. Whether you're up on a stage or not, you are really marketing yourself.

So, whether it be something as simple Attracting your ideal mate, stepping up in leadership or your career, earning more money or closing that big deal, your image says a lot about you. Your image says a lot, and with people, you have got nanoseconds to make that first impression. If you're going to show up and you've got an important message, which I know you all do, then you want to be at your absolute best.

Tami Patzer: *So, you said "nanoseconds." When somebody meets you, what are some of the opinions that they form in those couple of seconds, or seven seconds?*

Marcella Romoser-Scherer: Well, in the nanoseconds, they're going to decide whether they like you or not. It happens so quickly. I shouldn't say they like you, but literally, if they're going to continue the conversation, or if they're even going to want to engage with you. But, within 7 seconds, those 11 opinions are like, how successful you are, how educated you are, where your social status is, your trustworthiness, your level of sophistication, social and educational heritage, level of success, your moral character and even if they like and trust you!

When you think about it this way: we're all in sales, whether you like it or not, or you want to admit it. But, we are always selling ourselves, Or our ideas to others. whether it is an idea that you are presenting or, it could be like, "Hey, which movie are we going to see?" You are trying to get everyone on board to go to your favorite restaurant. It could be as simple as that! But when you're talking about strangers, and let's say you're going to a networking event and you're looking for potential customers, or you're going into a bank to apply for a loan, or you're going to close that multi-level deal.

Then, those opinions. You want them to get past all that so that they really listen to what they have to say, because most of it is visual first, before it is actually the words that you're saying, or what they're hearing. So, critical.

Tami Patzer: So, nanoseconds is like, they look at you and think, "Yes, I'll continue to check you out." Then within the next seven seconds, that's when they go, "OK, you're this, that and the other thing. I'm willing to give you more time, or not." Then of course, they look at how you present yourself. *You talk about working with* *people from the inside out, or the outside in. What exactly does that mean?*

Marcella Romoser-Scherer: Good question, I've worked with thousands of women, and a few good men, over the years using a series of questions, conversations and observations to help them determine what is important, how they see themselves and how they want to show up in the world and be perceived by others.

The way we adorn ourselves; the way that we dress is just an expression of who we really are and what we value in ourselves. So, we might as well show up in the best version of ourselves. I don't know about you guys, but my clients are smart and sometimes unclear about what their style is, or they lack confidence when it comes to pulling together outfit and frankly don't have the time, gift or want the hassle of trying to figure it all out.

And many of them are going to get on this stage and they have this really important message they want to say, and they just show up, instead of really thinking about that it matters. But it does. We want to align who we authentically are from the inside, out. I hope that makes sense. I've found, because I've done cosmetic makeovers for a really long time, I've found sometimes that just even a little bit of lipstick can make you feel more confident. Or, just wearing a pretty blouse, or whatever that might be. Sometimes, it's on the inside that we have to work on.

So, it's trying to align the inner and the outer beauties so it's authentic to who you are. Because when you show up authentically, then people really get you.

Tami Patzer: I really get that because, for example, color for me, I really like, I guess you would call them warm colors or cool colors. I like red, royal blue, purple, hot pink, magenta, those types of colors. And, I know for a fact that I am not a grey person, or a pale-colored person, or a beige, because of the way the colors make me feel.

I actually have kind of a cute little story. Back in the day when I was married, my ex mother-in-law gave me a grey coat. I wore the coat because it was warm, but I really didn't like it at all. Then one day, I forgot it at a Chinese restaurant. I never went back to claim it! So, that is an example, but it's exactly what you've taught. What I learned from you, Marcella, was to, number one, choose colors that make you feel good and that you look good in.

Can you talk a little bit more about that process you go through with someone in determining their style? Because, I'm the first to raise my hand to say that I don't really know if I have a style, or how to incorporate it. Because, number one, I do live in Florida, so it's hot. So, I look for cool, comfortable yet professional clothes and I need to be able to wear it with comfortable shoes. Those are kind of my personal criteria, but sometimes that doesn't match with the level of who I want to project. Because I obviously want to project that I am somebody who is professional, and put-together, and intelligent, as well as a high-class person. And I also want to elevate myself so that's what people see. *What are some things I could do to show that I am somebody they should pay more than seven seconds to?*

Marcella Romoser-Scherer: Oh, gosh, you've got some great questions here. And that's why I came up with the seven-step system of upscaling your image. The "S" stands for "Style" and "Silhouette" defined, because when we know what our style is, just think about it. Like you said, you've got criteria; we all have criteria. And let me just sidebar on this, is that you don't have to spend a million bucks to look like a million bucks. You know what I'm saying?

I am the biggest clothes horse probably on the planet. I worked on wholesale, so I was always able to get amazing things at wholesale prices, so I always appreciate the value of what you can get for the dollar. When I first moved to South Florida almost 30 years ago and started my business, I had absolutely nothing. So, I would go to Palm Beach to the consignment stores and I would buy gently worn clothing that I could afford, and that looked really great.

For those that may be starting, find that criteria, like Tami just said. You have to think about the weather, and who your audience is, and what you're aspiring to do. Also, you have to factor in what your budget is, because we'd all love to go to Neiman Marcus all the time, but maybe our pocketbooks aren't going to agree with that because we need to build a new website.

So, back to your question around style and how to define it., I do this really fun workshop. It's called "The Million Dollar Style and Vision Board". It's sort of like making a Pinterest board for yourself. It's a vision of what you want to step into, and it's about aligning yourself with what really resonates with you. You and I were talking about how, educational? What was the word that you described your style before we started?

Tami Patzer: Oh! Academic. My style was very academic.

Marcella Romoser-Scherer: Academic, yes. OK, academic. So, we can soften that word with like, classic tailored. You can think of Jackie O. Barbara Bush, or any of our president's spouses, like

Michelle Obama, they all have that kind of tailored, timeless classic kind of look about them.

Tami Patzer: I like that.

Marcella Romoser-Scherer: Yes, so, gee, you fit into the first ladies. But then there's some that, I've been giving the example that for this season, we're seeing a lot of flowers, and floral prints, and more flowy fabrics which would be more of a romantic style. But if you've ever noticed that you have items in your closet that maybe still have the tags on them, or maybe you've never worn them before, chances are pretty good either:

> **A.** The color isn't right
>
> **B.** The style is really not you, like, for example, that flower-printed blouse that's hiding in the back of the closet.
>
> **C.** It just doesn't fit you well

So, go look in the back of your closet those things, and you can kind of identify what's not right for you, then you probably see a theme of what is.

Tami Patzer: *So, just give me a little teaser here, what are some things I could do to look 10 pounds thinner?*

Marcella Romoser-Scherer: Well, good question. So, one of the easiest things is to wear a different neckline, for example, if you had a turtleneck as opposed to a V-neck blouse, it's going to elongate. And again, it depends on what your facial shape is and your physique, but definitely wearing more of an open neckline is one. Wearing color from head to toe, it doesn't necessarily have to be black, and I will tell you that it is a fallacy, that black will automatically make you look slimmer.

It could make you look older, because not everyone looks good in black. Believe that or not, but it's true. It can make it look like you have dark circles and shadows on your face when really, a lot of people think that it does make you look slimmer. So, beware. Head to toe color, wearing the same shoes, pants top or skirt from head to toe is definitely a great one.

You can also use accessories to elongate your look, whether it be an oblong scarf, or even a necklace that draws your eye up. So, it depends a lot on your body shape. Some of us can wear a belt, and some do not. A belt can cut you in half in some cases. So, keeping it simple, doing the monochromatic is excellent, and then drawing your eye up to your face are just a few.

Tami Patzer: *So, monochromatic, is that black and white, or is that any type of two-tones? Or am I misinterpreting?*

Marcella Romoser-Scherer: Actually, it's one color from head to toe.

Tami Patzer: Oh, "mono" meaning "one". I don't do it like I used to, but I used to wear black all the time; solid black. Now, it's mainly just the black pants, then I wear a colored top and then a solid jacket, or a blazer. And of course, the reason I like that is I also watch the style of my blouses, because I don't like my arms to show, so I found that there are certain cuts of clothing that do have sleeves but give you a shape.

And I'm heavier, but I also found that wearing clothes that fit me make me look better, than if I wore baggy clothes.

Marcella Romoser-Scherer: Yes, absolutely. I have an amazing tool I use for my clients that is literally based on your bone structure. It's not based on your size, it's based on proportions. So, it really is one of my secret weapons.

Tami Patzer: That's a good secret weapon, because that's the thing that I think most of us don't realize, is that there are people who have what I call "B. I". And it comes natural to you to look at someone and say, "Yeah, this type of fabric, these colors, these shapes go with your bone structure, your hairstyle, how tall you are." Because most of us, it's just like anything: if you're not educated in it, you really don't know.

And so many people try to buy the things that are in fashion, but they really don't work on someone. Something that looks great on someone who is a size double zero, isn't going to look good on a size 12 or 14 average woman, so that's always interesting. You said something that I thought was interesting.

You talked about the colors, and the fact that you could alter your clothes. Do most people, when they go to buy clothing, do they even think about that? Sometimes I'll go to Dillard's, and on January 1st of every year, they have this big super sale where it's like 50% off of 50% off, and it's a really good sale. Often, they'll have these really beautiful dresses, or pants.

What can you get altered? I guess that's really my question. When you go to the store, *If you, let's say, find a jacket that just hangs like a bag, could you get that altered? How do you know if that piece of clothing is something that could be altered, or if it's worth being altered?*

Marcella Romoser-Scherer: Yes, everything can be altered, but whether it's worth it or not; that's the essential question. So, recently I think I mentioned it to you that mentioned it, I purchased a beautiful designer, it's a couple thousand-dollar dress. More than that, actually. And it was on a crazy, crazy sale, but it totally did not fit me on the bottom. I'm, like, almost an upside-down triangle body shape, and this dress was for the opposite, a triangle or pear-shaped body, but the top fit me fine.

So, I based my decision on:

- The quality of what it was
- The color
- The majority of it fit me well, but it just needed some slight modifications

Because I kind of have a feel of what it costs to alter it, I was able to factor that cost into the price of the dress and knowing that for just a little bit more money, I was going to be able to have a timeless classic item that I could have in my wardrobe for a long time. So, that's what you want to ask yourself. As a matter of a fact, you guys can go to my website, and on there I have the 10 questions to ask yourself while shopping.

That's definitely something to factor in when you're purchasing anything new. So, when you try it on, you can ask yourself those 10 questions and definitely think about, "Does this need to be altered?" and "Would it be worth the extra money to spend to do it?"

Tami Patzer: Great, it's so funny because I'm at your website, and it's http://www.MarcellaScherer.com, but Marcella, you have a sense of humor that comes out on your website, even though you're an upscale image consultant. But I love, there's a photo on her website and it says, "Free Guide: 10 Questions to Ask Yourself While Shopping", then there's a tee-shirt that says, "I have nothing to wear, " and there's a pile of clothes.

And, I know that this is a true statement. I'm one of those people because, the other day I opened up my closet and there's all these clothes hanging there, I looked at them, and I go, "When did I buy that? WHY did I buy that?" And, "That is icky and not my color and I should just put it in a plastic bag and haul it to the Goodwill or something." Because, it will hang there for years and years.

It is funny when you find the clothes with the price tag. Maybe you bought it - and I do have things like this - 10 years ago, and it's never been worn. Then I have other clothes that the poor things are worn out because I wear them all the time, because they've become my go-to. So, I love that. But definitely, get that free guide!

Another thing that you have on your website that I just think is really cool, and I love this because, sometimes you go to websites and they're not usable; they're more like just a brochure. But your website, every single blog post is functional, actionable and usable information. Like, you have "The 5 Top Mistakes People Make When They're Coordinating Their Outfits, and How to Avoid Them". Everybody needs that!

"The 5 Core Pieces of Clothing You Need in Your Closet", " How to Declutter Your Wardrobe". I like this one, "Why Organizing Your

Closet by Category is Crucial for Your Speaking Success". I definitely want you to answer this a little bit, because I know a lot of people listening to the show are either entrepreneurs, professionals, c-suite executives, or speakers, or people whose primary goal is to speak either online, or normally on the stage.

So, can you give us just a few little tips about this closet organization by category? What are the categories?

Marcella Romoser-Scherer: Well, to me, and it may be obvious for some people, but think about this: have you ever gotten a last-minute invitation to speak, whether it be online, or at a networking event?

Tami Patzer: Yes! I actually have. It's like, "Tami, show up at 3 o'clock!"

Marcella Romoser-Scherer: Yes! So, that's my second step in the upscale: "Prepare for Performance, On and Off the Stage". Because, you never, never know when you're going to have this awesome opportunity to show up, and show up well so that people know, like and trust you. So that they want to either book you, buy from you, love you, whatever it is. So, your closet has to be prepared. And so, if you think about it, when you walk into your closet is it overwhelming? Is it easy for you to get dressed? Can you get dressed in three to five minutes if you got that call, put something together super quick and get out the door?

Because, I know that you're going to really be thinking more about "What the heck am I going to talk about?", or, "Do I have everything, my PowerPoint ready or whatever it is that you are going to deliver in your speech?" You're not really going to want to worry about what you're going to wear. It takes away from it; that's one more thing you have to be stressed out about.

So, by having your closet organized, and having it put into categories, literally you can step in there and you should be able to pull a couple of different things out and put it together and show up in a competent way. If you don't then I have a virtual wardrobe app for my preferred clients that is sort of like a personal Pinterest that has outfits coordinated for you, so that you can reference them on your phone.

Tami Patzer: So, they're your clothes?

Marcella Romoser-Scherer: Yes.

Tami Patzer: Oh, my goodness, how cool is that?

Marcella Romoser-Scherer: Yes, it's amazing.

Tami Patzer: So far, you've given us the steps of your Upscale system. I want to ask you briefly, with the other parts of your step program, because I do know that if they go to your website, like I said, your website has more real, usable information than I've seen. And I've looked at a lot of websites, because I used to make websites for people, and I love the fact that every single post has got real meaning, juicy information.

That somebody can go to your website and get, like if they have a speaking engagement at 9 o'clock in the morning and they have to have to go somewhere at 7, they can go to your website and get enough information to put a plan together and show up better than they could have without you, just from your website. So, just think if they actually get to talk to you!

Marcella Romoser-Scherer: Oh, gosh, well thank you, Tami! Because, I'm sure anybody that has a website knows it's an ongoing process and it never seems like it's good enough for you, so I'm glad you see a lot of value, and that there's some good content there. That's the whole idea.

Tami Patzer: It's really good content, and like I said, I've seen a lot of websites, and you provide great, added value. I bet if I looked at your website stats, I'd go, "Man, people hang out there a long time." because there's so much good information. *So, what would step number three be?*

Marcella Romoser-Scherer: Number three is the "S", and that's "Style" and "Silhouette" defined. We talked a little bit about that. And then, do you want me to go through the rest of the steps?

Tami Patzer: Yes, I would.

Marcella Romoser-Scherer: Ok, so number 4 is "Choose Your Colors". I'm a huge advocate about color. We talked a little bit about it, but knowing what your best wardrobe, hair and makeup colors are is really a game changer. No matter what your age, or even if you've had it done before, it's always a good time to revisit it. If you've had it done many years ago, revisit it. Because what I find is, it serves as a filter.

If any of you like to go to the sale rack, whether it be something like T.J. Max, or Nordstrom's rack, or whatever, you've already eliminated half of the clothes by knowing what your best colors are. That's number one. Number two is that it'll make you look younger, you'll have a glow. Like you, you were already getting the compliments that you got just by making that one little shift. But the other thing is that it helps you, we talked about organizing your closet, not only by the categories, but by colors.

So, you can think of a rainbow. If you really stick with colors that are in your season, then everything starts to mix and match together. For example, let's just use really easy neutrals, if you have black items: black shoes, black handbag, black jacket or pants, whatever. You've got to have those other items that make it work. If you have brown, or cream, or camel, now you've got to have beige, or tan, or different accessories.

If really, truly, one is better than the other, why not stick with the one that is best suited for you? Then, you just saved yourself so much time, money and effort with this whole other category that really doesn't serve you. It's going to save you time, it's going to save you money, you're going to look younger, you're going to love shopping a lot more because you've got a plan to get in there. That's number four, is choose your colors.

So, I do that through professional color analysis where we take fabric drapes, and I do a professional makeover. I have you bring your makeup kit, so we can go through it, because not all browns or natural makeup is created equal. We have to sift through those and pull the things that make you look young and healthy. So, colors are big.

Number five is "Attack the closet". For this step is also, I have a whole seven-step system for attacking the closet. There's a famous book, maybe some of you have read it, it's "The Life Changing Magic of Tidying Up".

She sold six million copies, and it's a fabulous book, you should read it. But she talks about, energetically, how everything that we have, that we own, whether it be in your closet, a drawer or anywhere, when it takes up an unnecessary space, that means you don't have room to bring something new into your life. Whether it be new clothes, or an item, to a relationship or new job.

If you think about that, if we have stale stuff hanging out in our closet, that's really not going to be good for anybody. So, get rid of what doesn't serve you. Get rid of things that don't fit you, that don't make you feel beautiful; get rid of it. Because when you do, you're going to feel amazing and it's going to allow, energetically, for new things to come into your life. That's a big thing.

Tami Patzer: That's really good advice.

Marcella Romoser-Scherer: Yes, isn't that great?

Tami Patzer: Yes, "The Life Changing Magic of Tidying Up", then from Marcella, apply it to your closet, to your clothes. And I think you're right, because it always gets me. The fashion right now, whoever wants to go back to the 70s? Why do they keep recycling the 70s? Because that's when I was a teenager. It didn't look good on me when I was 17, I'm pretty sure it's not going to look good on me now.

I just think that's so funny, because I do notice the recycling of fashion, every now and then I'll find something. I have a blouse that

I've had for 25 years, but it's a classic top, and it was a high-quality top, so it never faded. It still looks good today, even though I've had it for 25 years and worn it over and over and over again, but I just think it's funny because it's just a simple, classic top.

But, it was very high-quality, so it didn't fade. But then there's other clothes like the Gauzy stuff, the stuff from the 70s that I wouldn't buy now. Number one, because I'm too old; it's not my style anymore. But if I did, it would end up hanging in the closet, taking up that unnecessary space.

Tami Patzer: *So, you've gone through step five. Are there two more?*

Marcella Romoser-Scherer: If you have blouse that's 25 years old, it may be time to revisit. But here's what I want to bring up, because there may be some listeners also. But you have something that you absolutely love, and it's really hard to part with. OK, maybe it's nostalgic, that's one thing. You can take a picture of it, and you can still release it if you're good with that. But, if there's something that really fits you well and it is classic, you can take it to a tailor and they can make it; use that almost like a pattern.

Tami Patzer: Oh, that's a good idea.

Marcella Romoser-Scherer: Yes, because after that many washings and stuff like that, things are going to peel and they're just not going to be the same, no matter the quality. Anyway, I just wanted to add that in.

Tami Patzer: It's probably stretched out, but I was just amazed at the color because, it is funny when you say things that are nostalgic. Because, I'll tell you, when I first got it, it was obviously in the 90s. It was a top and then I wore it with a pair of blue pants, so I was that mono, the one color. I remember my daughter saying to me, "Mom, you look like a big blue crayon!"

It does a funny little thing. I don't wear the blue pants, obviously, those are long gone. But the top is still around. I just think that's funny. *So, what was number six?*

Marcella Romoser-Scherer: OK, number six is "Learn to Shop and Love It". I would say the majority of my clients do not like to shop. Or, I have a new client who loves to shop, but she has this habit of buying stuff because it's a really awesome deal.

Tami Patzer: Guilty!

Marcella Romoser-Scherer: All of us love to do that. Like, "I can't NOT buy this, because it's such a great price!", or whatever. But, a lot of it, in her case, ends up staying in the closet with the tags on them. So, no matter what the price is, if you're not going to wear it doesn't matter. You know what I mean? So, you want to learn how to shop. I already gave you tips around knowing what your best colors are, because now you've filtered through half the sales rack because you know most of those things aren't going to look good on you.

I have a strategy that I work with my clients, where we go into their closet, we pull out those key components that do work. Then, we make a shopping list so that when you go to the store, instead of just as a whim, "Oh, this is cool, I'm going to buy it.", You can really be more strategic in adding things to your closet that literally will work for you. So, back to when you get the call at the last minute to go to a speaking gig, now instead of just having a bunch of stuff in there that maybe looks good or not, it doesn't necessarily go together, it's going to take you a lot longer to fill in those pieces.

But when you have a shopping list and you're strategic, then you're going to love shopping because you've got a plan, and you know it's going to work, and you're going to get the results that you want. Right?

Tami Patzer: Yes. That's really cool. It's funny because I'm listening to you, and like I said, I watched your presentation, then the next time I went shopping, I used that color suggestion: "Know what your colors are". And I was able to eliminate. It's funny because, these tips that you provide, once you understand them and know them, they become part of you.

So, when you do go shopping, you're absolutely right. The other day, they had some clothes marked way, way, way down, like a couple of dollars. And it was like, "Oh my gosh, this is such a good deal." But I did exactly what you said. I said,"Well, number one, is it my color: yes or no?--No." Would you ever wear it? "No."

So, I walked away because I applied what I learned in that one, simple presentation that you did. All I can tell you about your speaking engagements is, obviously, they must be extremely powerful. Because I'm still, this was in about three months ago, or four months ago that I witnessed this. And here I am applying these simple rules, buying only colors that work for me, and saving money because I'm not buying things that I would never wear just because they're on sale. I'm guilty. To me, it's not a sale until it's like 75% off.

Marcella Romoser-Scherer: All of us appreciate a deal. But if you think about, it's like if you would make an investment, you think about the return on your investment. Right? So, you think about your clothes the same way. Even, think about shoes. You may have some shoes that you wear every day, or every other day. And then there may be these special shoes that you only wear on rare occasions.

Well, you have to think about the money. It's like getting a great haircut, it's the same concept. Why wouldn't you spend more to have a really awesome haircut? Or buy an incredible pair of shoes, no matter whatever the cost is. If you're going to wear them all the time, it's going to be a better return on your investment. You see what I'm saying? So, you can invest accordingly. That's why I was telling you about that designer dress that I bought. I knew it was going to be a classic piece, and it was an investment. But I knew it was going to be totally worth it.

Tami Patzer: Well, I think that is important. Especially because, if you want to be successful and, on your website, "Look like a million to make a million." In other words, if you want to make money, you have to look like money. You have to look like someone who's at a higher level. Even if you're just starting out, you have to project that image of success, so you can become successful.

I think everything you've been talking about, you're really saying it isn't difficult to spend wisely, and to choose wisely, and to make that investment in not only your clothing, but really, your clothing, your makeup, your hair, your image is an investment in you. And who better, or what better thing to invest in than your self-image so that you can become that successful person who you want to be? "When you look it, you become it." You know?

Marcella Romoser-Scherer: Yes, that is so true. When we upscale our image, we upscale our lives and we upscale the money that we attract, So, you have to look the part, you have to be the part. It's not a facade, but it's about you becoming and being that person. You're going to do, if you think about it, if you're going to make investments to expand your portfolio and you're meeting with a financial advisor, well, if they look like they've got scuffs on their shoes, maybe they don't have a nice manicure, or they're hair is unkempt, or they look in some way not all put-together, you're going to make assumptions.

Like: "Is this person detail-oriented?" "Are they going to do a good job managing my money?" They start to think about these little things because, the way you show up in one area of your life, is how you show up in all areas of your life. So, just saying.

Tami Patzer: No, I really do. Because the more you talk, the more I realize how important it really is to just start to pay attention. And, I'm guilty of sometimes not even looking in the mirror enough. I'll get the makeup on and comb my hair, but it's just simple things, like, before you get on stage, you'd want to look at yourself and make sure everything's together. And you don't have any wardrobe malfunctions.

I have lipstick on, and just simple little things. ***What is number seven?*** I think you've told me all of them except for number seven.

Marcella Romoser-Scherer: Yes. Number seven is: "Evaluate Quarterly". So, we talked about being "Prepared for Performance, On and Off the stage". And so, this is where, and I can use some of my clients as an example, Nancy Mathews, one of the founders of Women's Prosperity Network is one my clients. I style her for her big

Un-Conference event once a year, and I remember the first year that she hired me.

She wanted to get together like, two weeks before the event to go shopping, because she was super busy planning. It's a big deal, this is a five-day event that she does. So, I was like, "That is so not going to work! We have to plan ahead of time." Because there's nothing, think about this, I'm sure you all have maybe had an important event that you were going to speak at, or maybe you had a wedding or Bar Mitzvah or something that you were going to.

And what do you do? You wait until the last minute, then you go out and you're searching for that perfect thing, and you can't find it, and you're really stressed out. So, you either just suck it up and you just pay a lot of money to buy something that maybe isn't that great, but you have to have it because you don't have anything to wear. So, I always say plan ahead. It takes time to look good. We have to take care of ourselves.

It's part of being organized, you have to plan ahead. Same thing in your business, it's not like your website's going to suddenly be up and running, you have to think through and plan things out, and see what you have. Part of it is knowing what events you have. If you're going on a trip, what kind of things are you going to need to pack? Have you gained or lost weight and nothing fits right anymore?

A lot of my clients have multiple sizes in their wardrobe, and that's part of being female. So, we need to think about all those things when we start putting together our plan or thinking about shopping, or whatever. Do we have what we need to be able to function in our life? To make our life easy, and be able to dress with ease and confidence?

To show up in the best version of our self? That's really what the "Evaluate Quarterly" is all about.

Tami Patzer: Well, I know that's a fact. Because I know, there's been times where people will lose weight for some special event, then they're up to the last minute, those few pounds. And then, of course, they don't have anything to wear because they didn't start figuring that out until the last minute. Tell me a little bit more. We talked about it a couple of times through the conversation where people can find out more about you and what you're doing.

Tell me again where people can make contact with you. And also, you have some big events coming up, and this will air, probably right around the time of these big events. So, go ahead and tell me again where we can find more about you, and your website again. *But, tell us more about these events you're doing, because those are fascinating, what you're doing in these live events.*

Marcella Romoser-Scherer: My website is www.MarcellaScherer.com. I've got some free gifts on there, I've mentioned a few ways that you can get some great insight around style and color. Or, "The 10 Questions to Ask Yourself While Shopping", so go check that out. You can also email me at Marcella@MarcellaScherer.com. So, if you want some more information, or to find out a little bit more about how I work with my clients, or whatever I can do to serve you.

If you'd like me to come speak, or do something else, then reach out. I am active in the South Florida area and travel to events across the country and internationally speaking and doing joint venture projects targeting leaders, speakers, entrepreneurs and executives.

You can also go to my fan page on Facebook, and I've posted information about the events there. That's http://www.facebook.com/marcellascherer.

So check that. Then, the next event I have is "The Million Dollar Style and Vision Board Event", which I mentioned earlier.

And, that will be super fun. It's about creating the vision of what else is possible for you, really identifying what your style is. You're going to leave with a tool that will help you do a lot of the things that we've discussed here about stepping into your authentic style, in confidence, with ease.

And also, we're going to give some great tips on being healthy, because we want to feel good also. So, we've got all kinds of great things in store. And I'll also be doing a live makeover there to give you tips and tricks on how to update yourself instantly for the season and look your best. We're going to have a lot of fun.

Tami Patzer: I'll say! That just sounds wonderful! I love that, the concept of the vision board and style. Because, a lot of times people have heard about vision boards, but they don't quite understand how it could work. So, that's a perfect opportunity to learn how to use your vision board, and then actually use it for Creating your authentic style at the same time. Because, obviously, when you're healthier, and you're looking good, and your clothes can reflect all kinds of things.

Marcella Romoser-Scherer: I'll never forget, there was a movie on Lifetime or Hallmark where this woman helped this guy with his look. And, he went from being this dowdy accountant, to a good-looking accountant, basically. And it was all based on his clothing, and something as simple as a hairstyle, or changing the frames of his glasses. So, that's another thing. Men and women can benefit from the style, or restyling.

I just think that's very interesting about how just a little bit of education can turn things around and help you find clothing that looks good on you and fits you. Then, all of those options, like the fact that if you find something you like that is worth altering, that you can find a classic piece of clothing that can be part of your basic wardrobe so that you could jump.

They can literally go, "Can you be here to speak this evening?" And you can say, "Yes! Here I am." You're ready to go, because you've done this pre-work of organizing your closet with the tips that you gave and everything. So, Marcella, is there any one, last thing before I let you go that you'd like to wrap this up with?

Well, there is one other thing. I know we live, especially here in Florida, we live in a very relaxed kind of atmosphere. And, I was just out in L.A., and it's a very relaxed vibe. I don't want people's impression that you have to be "dressed up" all the time. So, when I say you want to make that great first impression, you could be in your jeans, or whatever. Just be pulled together. You know what I'm saying?

When I go to the gym, I don't put a whole bunch of makeup on or Fuss about my appearance. I just buy cute workout clothes that are nice, and not shabby and falling apart, and in my best colors And, I might put a little bit of lipstick on, or try to at least comb my hair. Because you truly never know who you're going to meet, or who that one person could be for you.

You guys have heard "The One Philosophy" from Nancy Matthews is that you just never know who that one person could be or who they would lead you to.

So, be prepared for performance on and off the stage, you never know. So, that don't mean you have to be a "Glamor Puss", but it does mean that you want to pay a little more attention. The last thing I want to leave you with is this: take care of this area of your life. It's really like self-care. It's a respect for you as a person, as a human, as a soul, that you are taking care of yourself. So, when you neglect that, it might show up in other ways of your life.

So, love yourself, be true to yourself, be authentic, show up in confidence, and you are beautiful no matter what.

Marcella Romoser-Scherer

Power up your wardrobe, image and inner confidence with Marcella's expertise to be the best version of you! No more confusion on what to wear or how to wear it and off the stage. Marcella has a passion to help you look and feel amazing and has powerful tools to align your inner and outer essence to convey an image and a message with your presence that is authentic and congruent with you! A message that gives you an UPSCALED and memorable first impression that will attract all you desire!

Marcella has over 28 years of experience in the skincare, makeup, fashion and leadership coaching industries. She will help you to identify your own unique style with determining your fashion personality, body type, face shape, most flattering hair, makeup and clothing colors and so much more. She is a national speaker, bestselling author, leadership and image coach as well as, a trainer in the direct selling arena. Not only is she an expert in her industry but has a team of consultants in the beauty industry and consultant nationwide.

Contact Marcella Romoser-Scherer:

TAMARA PATZER

Website: http://www.MarcellaScherer.com
Email: marcella@marcellascherer.com
Facebook: https://www.facebook.com/MarcellaScherer
Instagram: https://www.instagram.com/marcellafashionista/

Audrye S. Arbe

Audrye S. Arbe is a diversity expert, author, speaker, seminar leader, clairvoyant, wellness consultant, mystic intuitive, artist, healer, Mom, and Grammie. She counsels thousands of people worldwide. Born to make a difference. Audrye knows it all starts at home. This, plus being inspired by Source, had Audrye write her first book, THE MOTHER'S MANUAL, A Spiritual and Practical Guide to Child Rearing and Motherhood (TMM). Hailed as a masterpiece, THE MOTHER'S MANUAL is available on Kindle and as a PDF at www.AudryeNow.com, with 20 smaller books, birthed by the major work. WHAT IF? You Are and Life Is Miraculous!, ABC, Affirmation, Art Coloring Book, is printed on 100% post-consumer, recycled paper. The first printing saved eight trees. This delightful book is great for anyone five years young to 100 years and beyond, as the book transforms and uplifts the reader's vibration. The book's outstanding words and art pique the reader's attention and curiosity. Brain enhancement also occurs with the book's multi-perspective approach. Audrye's latest book, RAISING RACE CONSCIOUSNESS, Healing Racism, Sexism and Other Isms (RRC) is a PDF and Kindle book that is brilliantly written. A book for our time, RRC also has led to workshops, lectures and more. If you like to eat, check out VIM VIGOR VITALITY VEGAN!, Plus Enagic Kangen Water Specialties, PDF wellness and recipe book, at AudryeNow.com.

Vim, Vigor Vegan – The Three V's

Tami Patzer: Listen to this, Audrye has "VIM VIGOR VITALITY VEGAN!" plus "RAISING RACE CONSCIOUSNESS, Healing Racism, Sexism and Other Isms" available. She is an artist and owns Audrye OmArt: Art That Opens the Heart. She heads GoddessHeart LLC, and Achee.

This is what Audrye has said about coloring: "It's the new meditation, hailed by psychologists as a way to uplift depression and help those in recovery. This book, in particular -- WHAT IF? You Are and Life Is Miraculous! -- brings forth gales of laughter. It's ideal for children, adolescents, teens, and adults. All love this book."

Audrye is a born New Yorker who now makes her home in South Florida. She adores music, drums, raw vegan food. Audrye also loves spirituality, transformation, dancing under the stars and sharing with others. You can check out AudryeNow.com, A-u-d-r-y-e-N-o-w.com, to learn more and participate with Audrye in seminars, classes, groups, and in private sessions. Welcome Audrye!

Tami Patzer: Let's just say that you are a fountain of information because it's like oh my goodness, the books that you've written and the books that you bring to us are just amazing. So, let's go ahead and start with an overview. Let me know more about who you help.

Audrye Arbe: I have private clients, in terms of me as a clairvoyant, healer and metaphysician. I'm an energy healer. Most people have heard of Reiki; I'm Reiki Master. Although I'm a natural-born channel, and, yes, I'm born this way, I also study. It's a continual process. The people who choose to grow and evolve, whoever they may be, are my clients. When the younger ones come to me, I call them zygotes; they are often so open.

It's a real pleasure to see a bunch of people in their 20s already interested in their growth and development. The sessions I do are channeled, so I never know what's going to come up. It's such a pleasure to be able to support them (my clients) by showing them how to circumvent a whole bunch of junk, and they get really clear on the purpose of their lives. They learn how to create their life in a new way.

In terms of the art (Audrye OmArt: Art That Opens the Heart), the art is such fun, I have to tell you. They start with an Om, "Oooommmmm," an Om. Then I go from there. I meditate before I do any of this stuff. Source shows me something I am to create. The art is usually brilliant color, abstract, and can be looked at in any direction.

The books. Oh gosh! The books. I'm a natural-born writer, and I'm finally, finally, really bringing this stuff out, and it's pouring out of me. It's designed to create shifts and transformations in people and because ... Let's just say I can have a wild sense of humor that's already built in. "THE MOTHER'S MANUAL" has at least 24, full-color, pictures in it. People get the art with the book. With "WHAT IF? You Are and Life Is Miraulous!", that's the coloring book. It's got from A to Z pictures that anyone can color, from the kids who adore it to seniors. Seniors are buying the book for themselves and teens buy the book. "VIM VIGOR VITALITY VEGAN!" is not a coloring book, but it does have some really cool pictures. "RAISING RACE CONSCIOUSNESS," which I am thrilled is out now, has one playful piece of art in it that anyone can enjoy. It'll be a black and white piece so if people want to color it, or just look at it, the art will be there for them to do whatever they want with it.

My books are what soul, spirit, Source, God/dess, whatever word we want to use, prompts me to write. They come right out of my heart and soul and they are, generally, about something that is needed on this planet and that will appeal to people, so people can actually have a full, healthy, life physically, mentally, emotionally, spiritually, energetically, and, yes, financially.

Tami Patzer: So, let me ask you ... I want to go a little bit deeper with some of your books. The one that's maybe a little bit lighter would be the coloring book. The "WHAT IF? You Are And Life Miraculous." Let's go ahead and talk a little bit more about that. You do say that, right now, coloring books are really, really, hot. You actually talked about how coloring is the new meditation. If you want to go a little bit deeper on that. And then I really want to ask you more about "RAISING RACE CONSCIOUSNESS, Healing Racism, Sexism, and Other Isms" because right now, the world really needs this book. So, start with the lighter side, with the coloring book, and we'll go into some heavier stuff.

Audrye Arbe: It was a psychologist who said this. When I wrote the book, I had no idea this was some kind of hot ticket. I just knew it needed to be out. I'm born under the Sun Sign of Cancer. We are natural moms and nurturers. I'm born that way. So, my first book was for the mothers and it could be for the fathers: "THE MOTHER'S MANUAL." Okay. That book, by the way, comes with a guarantee. Read the whole book, and do at least two of the exercises, and I totally guarantee that the reader will grow.

Then I said, "Well, we need something for the kids."

I came up with "WHAT IF?" because I had a slew of these adorable, funny, little black-and-white pictures I had made some years ago. I'm laughing, going, "Who in the world made these?" They're so adorable.

Well, I did. Well, Source coming through me did that. I thought, everyone needs to know how to speak. So, I put together this book. I'll read you, for instance, some of the A words. We'll start with the first letter of the alphabet, A. Actually, let me just start with the first page of the book, which has brilliant color in it.

"What if? What if you are made of love and starlight? Possibility and miracle? Impossibility and divinity? Energy and matter? What if?! You can be whatever your heart chooses. Whatever you can image, sense, intuit, create, build, collaborate, know, and believe."

It goes on. Then we can come to the A words. My graphic designer did an awesome job. I did the art, I did the words, she did the ABC's and the design of the book. So, the A is called, Astronomically Always and then here we go.

"What if you are absolutely adorable, able, ancient, alight, astounding, atrocious, assertive, astronomical, and amazing?" When I've done this with kids, at events, and I look at them and ask, "Are you adorable?" They go, "Ahhhh!" Then I go, "Of course you are. Are you amazing?"

Their eyes get big, and I go, "But you are. You are totally amazing."

I haven't called them atrocious because I don't know these kids that way. We have had some truly unusual made-up words. With words like "atrocious," they, kids, teens, adults, can take it and correct it, but if we don't embrace all of who we are, then we can't shift anything.

There's even a time and place, now and then, to be a little bit atrocious.

And the art. The art is funny. The art's really cute. The kids look at it and love it and some of them don't even want to color it. Then they get the zeal to color and they come up with these gorgeous, gorgeous, gorgeous, renderings. At some point I'll do something with that. I'll do some kind of contest, but that's down the line.

The reason it's printed on 100% post-consumer, recycled paper is I love that, according to GreenPressInitiative.org, about 30 million trees are used to make books sold in the United States every year. Many of that is sourced from endangered forests. This equals 1,153 times the number of trees in New York's Central Park. That's a lot of trees. Deforestation accounts for 25% of human caused CO_2 emissions, which contributes to global warming. Virgin paper accounts for nearly 40% of the waste stream. I couldn't be part of that. I can't. I won't. That's why my books are either on Kindle or PDF because it's easier for me to get out to people. When I'm in the financial condition I need to be to print them all, then I will. I won't print on anything less than 100% post-consumer, recycled paper because I truly do love this planet and I have to be, for me to be able to live with myself, part of making the solution rather than any kind of problem. The PDF books come with a Certificate of Commendation, explaining why the book is a PDF and where to buy 100% post-consumer recycled copy paper, which is what I use.

Tami Patzer: Wow! That's really good information that you just provided about how many virgin trees are used up in just printing of books. I didn't know any of that and that's really logical. It does make a very good reason for getting books in a digital format because, of course, then you can save them and read them on your phone, on your computer, on your tablet, and you're not using any paper at all, at that point.

So, tell me more about "RAISING RACE CONSCIOUSNESS, Healing Racism, Sexism, and Other Isms." How did this particular book come up for you to write it? Why do you think it's so important to come out now?

Audrye Arbe: I actually started this book some gazillion years ago it feels like. I come from New York. I was going to do a seminar called Raising Race Consciousness. I took a look around and I thought, "We need this".

At the time I was really focusing on what we call race. The colorations of our skin and our look. Here I am, gallivanting around the city, and a lot of people are saying, "Well we don't need that. We don't need that."

I'm looking at them ... Remember I'm a psychic. It's really silly for people to say things to me that don't make sense because I'm going to see something different, deeper. Anyway, and then they said, "Oh that couple might need it because they are a quote, unquote, 'mixed-raced couple.'

I did do the seminar. Then I kind of tabled all that and then wrote "THE MOTHER'S MANUAL," and did all my healing books, and blah blah. Then it came time ... Now I'm in Florida and I'm on this book-writing journey right now. So, I pulled out my notes and realized it can't only be about race, it has to be about sexism, genderism, religionism, ageism ... What am I leaving out? Culturism, classism ... You name it, that's an ism. Okay? And ... I'm going to look to say this in a really elegant way. I'm somebody, my whole life, who has been inspired to live on the highest plane. Do I always succeed? No, I'm a person and I'm growing and evolving. Do I correct when I make a mistake? You betcha.

So, I will say that as a result of the 2016 presidential election… I am going to say this, so here we go. In the White House, in other positions, people I literally consider sociopaths that are traipsing all over the rights of human beings. That are looking to trash this planet and harm people.

So, this book, "RAISING RACE CONSCIOUSNESS" ... Remember I'm a healer. So, in this book we actually start with: What are we? I take it to, really, what are we? My premise is we're beings of light. We all come from Source, whatever you want to call Source -- God, Goddess, Allah, Great Spirit, Osun, Shekinah, Oludamare, Ein Sof, whatever someone wants to call it. Okay, the Great Beyond, the Field of Unlimited Possibilities, the Universe, all that. Many people can get stuck in ego and have a disconnect with their essence, a lack of awareness of deeper reality, as well as what I call dysfunctional ego, and they don't get anywhere. Anyone that I've ever met, including me, can have internal dialog, which is all that trash talk that goes on inside us. Stuff like "I'm not good, I'm too fat, I'm too thin, I'm too old, I'm too young, I'm too dumb, I'm too this, I'm not enough that."

All that. When any of us listen to that and operate from that, we harm ourselves and others. So, time to go beyond that. I address that stuff and I address the denied part of who any of us might be. In the book I've incorporated the entire seminar. In one way, shape, form or another, it's in there. Plus, plenty of other information from other people who have done amazing things, including Jane Elliott, Knellee Bisram, Prof Dr. Rhonda Magee, and other people. Know that there's not one group on this planet that has it all together. It isn't about this group or that group or the other group or this one's better, and that one's worse. None of that. It's all about each human being who reads the book looking within and seeing, through doing any of the exercises, or what pops up to them as they read, might need clearing and shifting.

So, it's done in a loving way because I'm a healer. Yes, now and then, and I've done my best to clear this, there's a little stick that wants to just poke a little. Like, "Look at this!" That's there, too.

We can all be operating on a higher frequency. I mean, I, frankly, have always loved, I just love that our species comes in so many colors and shapes and hair textures. I think it's phenomenal! I find that one of our biggest blessings. That some people have issues with that has always been a little strange to me, so I address where that can be coming from. Of course, I interviewed about seven different people and, I have their input and their take on it also. The book is meant to cause shifts.

I'd like to see it in schools. It's already out as a PDF and Kindle. As I'm funded, it'll come out as a printed book on 100% post-consumer recycled paper or something better. Other than that, it will be PDF and Kindle, and anyone will be able to get it. It's a very reasonable price, $7.17, and that's it. Is the book germane now? Oh yes, indeed! Very much so. Very much so.

Tami Patzer: *Your book, "RAISING RACE CONSCIOUSNESS, Healing Racism, Sexism, and Other Isms,", also has a seminar that you created that you have incorporated into the book. So, you talked about some exercises people can do?*

Could you just give me an example of maybe one or two of the exercises somebody might do while they're reading this book and working on themselves?

Audrye Arbe: Some of it would be looking at race, some of it would be looking at one's attitude about this sex or that gender, and so on. So, it will literally be ... People can write right in the books, okay? I recommend someone having a notebook, whether it's a paper notebook, or a computer notebook, or any other doo-dad that might work in terms of technology, okay? I'm still a paper and pen kind of person and I use as much recycled as I can.

So, say it's about race. There'll be a question for the person. No one's going to look at this. No one gets a grade on this. This is for someone to look at their own self. "What do you think of your own coloration? What do you think of your own racial status?"

They get to look, and they get to write. "What do you think, or feel, about somebody that looks different than you?" And they get to write. "What have you been shown about whatever it might be?" They get to mull, feel, think, write. Before we get to those parts, there's already been the chapters about, "What are we? What are we anyway? How have we been conditioned? Did we really start all over here on the Earth, or did we start somewhere else? What in the world are we?" As the people do this, they start to get in touch with some of what's going on inside them that they may never have perceived before. There are a lot of people who don't want to look at it. They think, "Well this is the way it is and that's it. End of story."

Without doing any self-examination, or self-healing, or "How do you feel when you see blah blah blah blah blah? What goes on inside you? Is this the way you'd like to stay? What can you do differently?"

Then I give ideas. If somebody goes through the various processes in the book, and I do recommend they do it, they will grow. How they will grow is up to them. How much they will grow is up to them. It's unlimited possibilities. If someone goes, "I don't want to grow at all," then they're probably not going to read my book. But if somebody goes, "I don't think I need to grow," and they start reading the book, they might have aha! moments.

My editor has said she'd like to see this in schools. She feels it would be good to some people who have some issues about who they are. The book talks about the different colors and how different people in a particular grouping, they have looked at the different colorations within that grouping and other groups. I address such things as white privilege and I define it. I address such stuff as black victimization. I address such stuff as quote, unquote, "I don't see color," which I think is funny and silly, and false. I address such stuff as light-colored black because to me there is no such thing. There's mixed-race! I address that whole concept. I address sexism. I address genderism. I address xenophobia. More of the focus is on racism that can be applied to all the "isms."

Why is it important? Look at the planet. Look at our country. Look at the way a lot of people still hold The Creator of All, by whatever language, whatever anyone may want to use, there are still many people who really think it's a He. It's a He!??!! I said to someone who I met on a plane, a really lovely woman. I said, "How could it only be a He? If all of that was only a He, there's no template for a She."

Yet, we have She's, and He's, and in-betweens – Ze's and Zhe's ? -- and stuff that we don't even know what's coming next. I mean this whole transgender situation and people is something that took me by surprise in terms of how many people are. So, we don't know ... I'm a psychic; I usually see or feel what's around the bend. We don't know what our species might be coming up with in the next 20-30 years. We don't know what's going to happen when we actually are on other planets. We will be. How we, as a species, may morph, in some kind of way, or not morph, or what kind of quality is going to be particularly important. We don't know which particular grouping of talents, gifts, and abilities, that already exist now, and we'll be flowering more, might help us get wherever we're going. What about blends of human and "alien" from other planets, times or what-have-you. We must be open, as we are not the only species in existence with consciousness.

I am a psychic, and I've seen clients now, professionally, for over 35 years. I did seminars in New York, and I do seminars here. I took classes, and stuff like that. I give classes. I've gotten to see that people have talents and gifts you wouldn't even believe. There are gifts that aren't written about because different people have them, who haven't been publicized. It has been my absolute blessing to be able to empower and encourage people with the gifts that they have because those gifts and people are needed. It's needed.

I had a client who hated her gift. She would have certain dreams sometimes. This particular kind of a dream would show somebody, and it was somebody she would know. These weren't common dreams. Within two or three weeks, couple of weeks, that person would pass from the Earth. She told me, "I hate that dream. That kind of knowledge That gift."

I told her it was a gift. She didn't call it that. I tuned in and advised her. "What are you doing with these people? Are you speaking with them?"

She said, "Nothing. I can't tell them they're likely to die."

I continued, "How about, since you know these people, you would have a conversation with them to find out where they are in their life and encourage them, in the most loving way, to create completions with everything because what you have is a gift. You can help prepare someone to transition. You don't have to tell them about your dream, if you choose not to."

She repeated, "I didn't want to keep the gift."

If someone really, really, really, really does not want to keep a gift, then you do a prayer and you ask Source for it to be taken away. Do I recommend that? No. However, it's a free choice. I had and have clients with gifts that are amazing. They were able, almost, to see beyond, through walls, make inventions that use techniques not yet available. Not just medical intuitive, and I have a some of that, but to just look at somebody and it's like an X-Ray and they can see what's going on with them. I mean what a wonderful gift that is!

So, there were many, many more. There are many more. I had people that, they could build things that don't even exist. Because I did readings for them I was shown stuff that I did my best to explain, and they understood what I was talking about. The particular gifts I would see in some of them, Divinity graced them in the here and now, and in the future, making things that no longer exist, that just don't exist yet and, yes, that's needed. Our species is amazing. Our abilities are outstanding.

In terms of race and race consciousness, for any group, ANY group, to think it's automatically because of its color, its sex, its sexual orientation, its religion, the country it's born in, the kind of money it has, it doesn't have, no. No, no, no, no, no. That is all distorted ego. We don't know who's got what gift and what ability that's going to be important. Never mind that we're all from the same Source. We're at different levels, that's for sure. There are older souls and younger souls. There are ancient souls. There's certainly more evolved souls and less evolved souls. We have to recognize that. It's foolish, in my personal opinion, to give a less evolved soul a lot of power if that person doesn't know how to handle it.

Tami Patzer: Makes sense to me, Audrye. It is so phenomenal listening to you and it seems to make perfect sense to me when you're talking about, raising, not only, race consciousness, but the racism, sexism, the gender, because it's so amazing to me how accepting so many people are of others and then how unaccepting other people are in the world. And how they just can't let go. Even when they see that they're wrong, it's like they can't let go of that. They'll fight for their wrongness-

Audrye Arbe: Yes. We call that cognitive dissonance. Willful ignorance. Dysfunctional ego.

Tami Patzer: And I see that a lot in the world today, that people won't back down. Even though they know, "Uh-oh. I think I made a mistake," they won't back down from that. So, I'm really looking forward to all of your books and, actually, your "WHAT IF? You Are and Life Is Miraculous!" coloring book. I want that book for my grandchildren. I have a seven and a 14-year-old. I just love the words and the fact that you can have this really positive conversation with children, and people of any age, while you're giving them these amazing, powerful words. They're not only learning about how wonderful they are, but they're learning a great vocabulary at the same time. Also, of course, the mission behind the book, being printed on

100% post-consumer, recycled paper. So, you've woven into every single one of your books, you've woven in these practical life lessons and thought-provoking things that will raise people's vibrations and consciousness and help them become ... I just got goosebumps, so I must be saying something that's true.

It's really amazing. *So, tell me, Audrye, where can we find out more about what you're doing now? And give me some ways to connect with you.*

Audrye Arbe: The new website is http://www.AudryeNow.com. It's up and growing. It will have all my art, books, seminars, speaking engagements, more. People can go to www.YouTube.com/AudryeNow also. Check me out on FB with the different FB sites for my four different books.

My other website is http://www.goddessheartwater.com. That talks about Kangen water, which is this special kind of alkaline, micro-clustered, anti-oxidizing water, that when people drink it, the Kangen water improves their body's alkalinity and true hydration. I'm a distributor for Enagic. People are getting healed of cancer and many other horrible conditions because the water creates changes in the body, and the body heals itself. This is real! I will give you my e-mail and I'll give you my toll-free number. I'm a real person. I have a cell phone.

Tami Patzer: I know you're real. I'll vouch for you Audrye. People know I'm real, so I'll vouch for you Audrye.

Audrye Arbe: That number is 888-757-3223. And the reason I have that is because it's 1-888-75-peace, P-E-A-C-E. I thought it was interesting. People can also reach me at 561.717.9965. My email is audryenow@gmail.com My Youtube Channel is AudryNow as well.

Tami Patzer: Okay. So, "audryenow.com" is the key to get hold of you. If you can just remember the A-U-D-R-Y-Enow.com and believe me, with this interview, your photograph will be seen so people will be able to match your face no matter where they find you. *So Audrye, is there anything you would like to leave our listeners with?*

Audrye Arbe: I want everyone to really know the Light Divine Love that we all have within us is always stronger than anything else. So, in the times we are in, no matter what is going on, and we can all be triggered, it is important to have a daily practice. Start the day with Breathing Attunements, lifting to the Light! Gratitude and Appreciation. Be the Light. It is vital that we lift our frequencies and live consistently on a higher vibration. I do this myself, absolutely. I do classes, sessions, speaking and seminars on this -- breathing techniques, meditation, releasing, reintegrating, and centering. No matter what it may seem like out there -- or in anyone's internal dialog -- the Light and Divine Love is stronger. We have to have that readily available within us, which we do, that we can tap into, and evolve. Everyone has this. Everyone. Bless you and thank you so much. A big hug to all the listeners and readers.

Audrye S. Arbe

Audrye S. Arbe is a cosmic being, diversity expert, clairvoyant, wellness consultant, mystic intuitive, artist, healer, speaker, seminar leader, Mom, and Grammie. She counsels thousands of people worldwide. Born to make a difference. Audrye knows it all starts at home. This, plus being impulse by Source had Audrye write her first book, "THE MOTHER'S MANUAL, A Spiritual and Practical Guide to Child Rearing and Motherhood," now hailed as a masterpiece. It's available on Kindle and as a PDF with its 20 smaller books derived from the main book. "WHAT IF? You Are and Life Is Miraculous!" is an ABC, Affirmation, Art Coloring book that's printed on 100% post-consumer, recycled paper, great for anyone five years young and beyond to 100+ years. All Audrye's books transform and uplift your vibration. 'WHAT IF?'s" multi-perspective art entertains as its outstanding and unique words pique the intellect, which leads to brain and consciousness enhancement. "RAISING RACE CONSCIOUSNESS, Healing Racism, Sexism and Other Isms" engages, teaches, shares, gentles, and, yes, may startle people with its clarity and honesty. Readers will evolve. "VIM VIGOR VITALITY VEGAN! Plus Enagic Kangen Water Specialties" created wellness with scrumptious recipes, including, yes!, raw organic cacao. Healthful and yummy chocolate!

Contact Audrye Arbe:

Website: http://www.audryearbe.com

Email: info@audryearbe.com

Heather Hanson

Heather is a life-long learner, educator, swing dancer and international travel enthusiast. She is devoted to her family, friends, and helping improve the community around her. She has 16 years of experience in education; both as English as a second language teacher, as well school administration.

She has a bachelor's degree in Intercultural Communications from Eckerd College, a master's degree in education from Radford University, and additional post-graduate hours from Nova Southeastern University. She currently works as a school administrator for two charter schools, RCMA Wimauma Academy and RCMA Leadership Academy. She's a Data Coach with Hillsborough County Public Schools, an avid swing dancer and an amateur model.

When in Pain – Dance

Tami Patzer: I'm really interested in your background because, number one, and I'll start with your hobbies, or avocations before I get into what you do on a daily basis. But, let's talk about the fact that you're an international traveler, you're a swing dancer and an amateur model. Every single one of those sounds like there's a story behind them. *So, tell me a little bit more about your background?*

Heather Hanson: I grew up in West Virginia; a very small town called Lewisburg, West Virginia in the Greenbrier Valley. I lived in the same house, had the same friends, up until graduation from high school, and then came to Florida for college at Eckerd College, which is a fantastic small liberal arts college. In the first semester, I met lot of people from different countries, and found out that Eckerd has a big focus on overseas studies as well as international students on campus, and the cross-cultural bug bit me.

I felt like my goal would be to live overseas and become bilingual, and I ended up being an English as a <u>S</u>econd <u>L</u>anguage teacher a few years later. I did some work in Istanbul, Turkey, and in Nagoya, Japan. I did a lot of traveling in Western Europe, and some other countries in Asia as well as in Mexico and Haiti.

Tami Patzer: Wow, that is an international background! *So, you were in Japan, and that's where you landed and actually started doing some heavy-duty teaching?*

Heather Hanson: Yes, I had done some other teaching before I landed in Japan, but Japan was the longest job I had when I was a teacher, as opposed to being an administrator. I taught at a two-year vocational college in Nagoya, Japan and I really enjoyed the culture there; I loved the food! And, I really became very passionate about Sumo wrestling. Nagoya is one of the cities that hosts the Sumo wrestling tournaments that only occur six times to a year. I studied the language - the written and the spoken language. And, I just had a really great time and really good social life.

Tami Patzer: *So, how did you end up coming back from Japan?* It sounds like you were really happy there.

Heather Hanson: I was very happy there. I felt like I was living my life's dreams, which were, like I said before, to live overseas and work towards becoming bilingual. And, unfortunately though, I started having some trouble with my right arm and hand when paralysis that was difficult to define started occurring. I tried to go back to work and just work part time, while seeing doctors in Japan.

The pain, with time, spread throughout my body; and it was excruciating pain that made it difficult to even stand up, to even raise my arm above my head. Even riding a taxi in Japan, the vibrations of that caused me more pain. After about three months of trying to go back and forth working part-time and then resting, I finally had to give it up. A doctor suggested I be placed in the hospital, and I ended up having to be in a Japanese hospital for two months under the care of an orthopedic surgeon who was, fortunately, fluent in English as well, because he studied in Pennsylvania.

Tami Patzer: *And then what?*

Heather Hanson: Then, part of the diagnosis, they were presuming, had something to do with the C7 area of my neck, which is called a cervical rib. Which, for some people, can be just an abnormality that is benign, but it seemed like it was causing a severe paralysis on my arm and hand that exercising the cervical rib might be a solution. So, with that presumption, they sent me to a teaching hospital in another city.

But that surgeon diagnosed me with <u>R</u>eflex <u>S</u>ympathetic <u>D</u>ystrophy, and said, "People with <u>R</u>eflex <u>S</u>ympathetic <u>D</u>ystrophy should not have anything happen that incurs more pain. Because your problem is, that you're pain mechanism has gone on overdrive, and is misfiring. It's the reason that you're in constant, severe pain, more so tha<u>n</u> the cervical rib. Exercising the area around the cervical rib isn't going to solve your problem. So, let's not do surgery."

That's that. They were very kind and generous at the hospital because, like I said, I stayed two months in an in-patient hospital. That's probably unheard of in the United States, just for having chronic pain. And, I left Japan at the end of those two months, and came back to the United States, in West Virginia, to stay with my parents, with the intention that I would somehow magically get well and return to a productive life of a young person who was excited about life, who had career goals, and had a master's degree and had interests.

But my body had other problems, and I just wasn't ready to quite go back to work. I spend several years seeking medical attention from multiple doctors in West Virginia, North Carolina and Florida with a lot of hypothetical diagnoses, but nothing really concrete and nothing would really help with treatment plans. Basically, I just lived with my family and tried to co-ordinate my medical treatments and medical appointments. And, I felt as if I had lost a lot of my passions in my life.

I had not lost my family, I had not lost my Christian faith. But, I had lost my social life, I had lost my interest in life: living overseas. I was living in a retirement town in Sun City Center, which was a very supportive place to live when you have a chronic pain or disability problem, but it wasn't giving me the right social interaction I needed as a young person in my early 30s. So, I was rather depressed.

Tami Patzer: So, obviously, something switched, or a light turned on, or you discovered something. Because today, you are actually swing dancing, and you're an amateur model. So, what did you discover, or what happened that helped you get to where, now, you're working at the two different academies, and you do have a pretty bright social life; what happened there?

Heather Hanson: It was a gradual process over several years' time. I think the first really important component of my healing process was being three weeks in a Tampa General Pain Clinic, an in-patient therapy program with focused physical therapy, occupational therapy, psychotherapy, and education to educate the whole person on how to deal with and manage chronic pain, and still move on with your life even though you might not be able to get rid of all the pain.

I also did a lot of meditation and hypnotherapy and had a lot of different people help me with those processes. I did other complimentary therapy modalities such as aromatherapy, magnet therapy, vitamin therapy, you name it, I probably did try it at one point or another. And, I just went very, very slowly. I went back to work at a job where I worked 10 hours a week; I worked there for eight weeks. After that, I went to a job where they allowed me to work 12-15, sometimes 18 hours a week; I did that for several years before I gradually moved to full-time.

Over that period of time, too, I also had a really wonderful boyfriend who was a best friend and boyfriend who is a stroke survivor, and he really was an inspiration to me, and a very good model for me in how to live my life with chronic disability issues, but still make every day count, and get up every day and be grateful for your life, enjoy all the interactions you have with the people that you love. He really modeled that very well for me.

Tami Patzer: Wow. So, of all the things that you did, would you see it really was a combination of all those things, or was there any one thing you did that seemed to really help with the pain management? Because you mentioned meditation, hypnosis, vitamins, exercise; it seemed like you did a lot of different things.

Heather Hanson: I believe it was a combination of all those things. Accepting the gradual process; accepting that it was a process of pacing myself, setting some goals but not too high, pushing myself but not pushing myself too hard. Because any time I would push myself too hard, I would often have setbacks. And the setbacks sometimes lasted weeks, or even months. Sometimes, even years. I was in two car accidents in 2011, for example. And, that set me back several years.

Tami Patzer: I see. So, in 1996 is when you started to have the issues? And this is of course 2017 as we record this, so this has been a long process. But the good news is, you obviously recognize, and you pay attention to when you are doing too much, so you know how to pace yourself. Tell me more about your passion for dancing.

Heather Hanson: That's a really, really big help for me when I feel a little bit less than able to do everything I want to do. Because occasionally I still have an urge to live overseas again, and I feel like I probably don't have a strong enough foundation in my health to live overseas again. Sometimes I feel little short changed, let's say. But, I try to make up for that with all the other passionate, interesting things I can do, and capitalize on that.

The dancing, I started in 2007, and I met up with a group of swing dancers in the Tampa area about participating dancers with a group called Swing Time, and they have weekly dances. I really had a lot of fun meeting people in a very casual, fun environment with people being very upbeat and positive just to get together, enjoy music, enjoy expressing your love of music through the dance. I just really had a lot of fun with that, and I very quickly turned into a party organizer.

Within about six months, I started organizing parties with a theme from a friend and getting people to dress up according to the them, sing karaoke-style, as well as dance, and dress up, and have a big party. So, I turned into a social leader within the swing dance community. Whether I could, say, get on a plane and go overseas again, or, whether I could run a marathon - I couldn't do those things - but I found out what I could do. I really love interacting with people, I like people around me to be happy. So, I just tried to create that.

Tami Patzer: So, you have the swing dancing bug. *Did you always know how to dance? What made dancing appeal to you?*

Heather Hanson: Dancing appealed to me because I grew up with a mother who is a dancing teacher, and she had a dancing studio for young girls that taught ballet, jazz, tap and gymnastics. And, she was the only dancing teacher in Greenbrier County at the time. In fact, there weren't any teachers in the neighboring counties, so she taught a lot of classes in dance to meet the needs of the young people who wanted to learn dance.

I started at three years old and would take a lot of different classes at the same time. If I wasn't taking a class, I was watching the other students take class because, after school, the dancing studio was my babysitter. She had two really large recitals each year, and what do you do at recitals? You put on costumes and you dance! So, I picked this up again in my adult life.

It's putting on a costume and performing, and it's just a real joy to entertain other people through music and dance, and costuming. I guess that's what I'm continuing to do in my 40's. It's just interesting that I wasn't doing that in my 20's and 30's, and I pick up things from my childhood and the influence from mother, here again in my 40's.

Tami Patzer: That is really interesting. And the fact that you like costumes and dancing, that makes perfect sense that now you're an amateur model. *Tell me more about that adventure.*

Heather Hanson: A friend of mine who owns a ballroom studio called "Dance Forever" in Clearwater, she was participating in a Meetup group and posting her pictures on Facebook. I've enjoyed those for about two years, and finally I just got up the courage to say, "Maybe I should try this out with you, Cathy." And, the Meetup group is based around photographers and amateurs who want to help each other out, and help build portfolios for each other, and just practice the skills involved in creating an interesting, creative image.

It's called "TaMPA," it's through meetup.com, and we just get together around a special location and theme, and the models can assemble their costumes however they wish, according to the theme. Usually it takes around two to three hours of time interacting with different photographers and creating different images. It's a really nice creative outlet for me. I feel like even recently, I was participating in one of these and I was in a lot of pain. And I haven't able to walk very well lately because of that pain; but still I was able to participate in a really fun TaMPA event at a western TV set.

It isn't currently used as a TV set but is definitely a TV set that was fully functioning at one time. I was able to participate for three hours just modifying the way I stood so that I didn't put too much weight on my left foot, came up with great pictures, had a super time and I didn't even need to tell anybody I was in pain. I like being able to capitalize on what I can do.

Tami Patzer: I think that really is very inspiring because, you're basically saying, "Hey, I still have pain. But I'm not going to let that stop me from living my life and having a good time." Like I said earlier, when you said that you recognize when you maybe are doing too much, so you can manage yourself along those same lines, wow, you've got such a fascinating background!

Your daily life as a teacher and administrator is also very interesting. *So, tell me more about RCMA Wimauma and Leadership Academies. Those sound very interesting, and tell our audience a little bit about where these Academies are, and a little more about that?*

Heather Hanson: It's a charter school, this is my 10th year as part of two charter schools on the same campus that are under the umbrella of a non-profit organization called "Redlands Christian Migrant Association" which is in its 51st year of existence in the state of Florida. It's well-known in the state of Florida for operating Head Starts and childcare centers, mainly catering to families who are migrant, farm working families or low-income Hispanic families that might not have as many choices for the private childcare options.

This organization has about 60 or so centers around the state, and also three charter schools; and I'm an administrator of two of the three charter schools. We are very proud of the things we do to help young people see a brighter future for themselves and try to see education as a way to have more options in life, rather than just repeating the type of work that their parents have done, which is, usually in construction or agriculture. We have a relative amount of success. We have a lot of students who are accepted into special programs after they leave our school, because of their academic success.

We're very proud of what we do. I work with people who are very passionate about helping each and every child be successful, and we have a lot of support from the community. That's another thing I think is very special about our schools, is how much community support we have through volunteers, partnerships and grants. So, each and every day I feel like I see a miracle happen, and I think that is also something that keeps me happy and positive and puts a fresh smile on my face.

One day or two days, I might wake up feeling a little less healthy. Getting to school and seeing the children's faces, they're so appreciative of what we do at school, knowing the community is behind our schools, knowing that I work with people who really care, this surpasses any of my feelings I may have started my day off with about, "Ooh, that medication gave me a bad side effect and I don't feel so good." So, I feel like my recipe for living a happy, successful life has a lot to do with my job, feeling passionate and feeling able to contribute to my community through my work.

Tami Patzer: Wow! So, you work with a lot of migrant families. And for many of them, obviously, English is not their first language. *So, what's some of the things you do to help these people and their children?*

Heather Hanson: Well, one of the things we do is we have a lot of education within the school environment. We have a lot of things that are visually stimulating and use language to bring up those concepts of vocabulary in their environment. We use a lot of singing, and chanting. We know young people love singing and music, so we use those to help teach educational concepts.

We also have a lot of our people on campus who are bilingual, so that if the children do need that support from their home language, they have plenty of people to access for that. We believe that the children shouldn't forget their home language; that they build both languages at the same time. Then, they'll be stronger as an adult, or have more opportunities for jobs if they're bilingual, they'll have more opportunities to have relationships with people if they're bilingual. So, we don't want them to forget that. But at the same time, we want them to be strong in the English language.

We also invest a lot in extra-curricular activities and field trips. Our children average about five field trips a year, and we take them to local sporting events, local art shows, and performing arts events to get them exposed to different things in the community. Because, with our typical child, you ask them, "What did you do this weekend?" the response is either "Walmart," "Hang out with my cousins" or "Go to the flea market".

So, the next week, you ask them again, "What did you do this weekend?" and it's the same three options again, and again, and again.

To really see a future with unlimited possibilities, you have to see the world; you have to see what's out there. So, we invest heavily through grant writing to get the funds to take the children out in the community.

Tami Patzer: I think that you're absolutely right. And that's something that Eckerd College promotes - I also am an Eckerd *Co*llege grad - and that is something that I really got a lot out of from going to Eckerd College. And, you're applying that life-long learner concept out in the real world, and every day you're helping these children and their parents understand that not only is a good education about learning the basics of reading, writing and arithmetic, but it is about being multi-cultural, being out in the world.

I think you're absolutely right about being bilingual, because if you're able to communicate in multiple languages, it really is a door opener. Especially here in Florida where we have a lot of different languages that people speak. So, if you could speak, say, English and Spanish, that really does open a lot of doors. *Do you find that the children that you work with need a lot of support? Or what do you think is the most important thing for the children to learn about to help them develop a healthy self-esteem?*

Heather Hanson: We try to emphasize that you should set goals and reach goals. We also give them lots of love and acceptance, and we give them a lot of forgiveness. If they stumble with their behavior, we have some consequences, but we try to emphasize minimal consequences for their behavior. And, a lot of understanding, forgiveness, and talking through the issue with them. We also work really closely with the parents and have a good relationship with the parents and family, which is part of the whole picture of educating a child.

We have over 90% attendance at most of our parent meetings, and we have a lot of classes in the evening for parents on how to be a better parent, and how to participate in the United States educational system. Those classes are given in Spanish for the parents, because we want the parents to partner with us. We want the parents to see the school as a resource for them, and through the relationship you help a child move towards healthy self-esteem.

When the parents value education, which, culturally speaking, the Mexican culture comes from a background of respecting educators and respecting teachers. But even more so, we provide a lot of extra services for the parents in a partnership feeling to provide that co-operation between the parents, the school, and the child.

Tami Patzer: *Because you're used to working with people from multiple cultural backgrounds, what do you think some of the misconceptions that people have about these parents and children who are part of that migrant worker, or Hispanic, community?*

Heather Hanson: Well, I think that in our immediate community we're fortunate that I don't hear a lot of negative stereotypes. And like I said, we do have so many organizations that accept our grant applications and fund them, or partnership with us by bringing people on campus, or letting students go to something off campus to experience life. So, I feel that in our immediate area in Hillsborough County, I'm not experiencing a lot of negative bias.

But at the same time, I am from rural West Virginia, which, traditionally has had some bias against people who are from outside. And when I say from outside, I mean that there was some bias against people from Virginia, the neighboring state at times. So, the bias extends to people who are, sometimes, in other parts of our country, in some people's minds. One of the biases I think you might hear is that people from farm working communities are just, naturally, not able to learn much, maybe not able to do much more than their parents did anyway.

So, maybe a person might think that they can't go further. However, we have a very active GIFTED services program at our school, and we actually have 8% of our population being served in the Gifted program, whereas the traditional Florida school has about 4.5%. We definitely have children who can think out of the box and have interests that are very strong in different academic areas and can be served in the Gifted program.

We also have students who graduate from eighth grade and go into a program in a local high school that is a very competitive program, where they get to be in a dual-enrollment program with a local community college. And, they get to work on their high school diploma, as well as an AA degree at the same time. If these people who are from farm working backgrounds can be competitive and do that, I think that shows that they do have the ability.

It's just providing young people with the right set of circumstances, and love and support, and understanding. I like to believe that any child can succeed.

Tami Patzer: I think you're absolutely right, and you are an example of everything you're talking about. It's all about setting goals, and moving forward, being persistent, and also lifting others up, and helping them to take everything that they have to be a positive factor to improve their life.

You said that you had a 90% participation rate in your parent meetings. That is just phenomenal that the parents are there supporting the children. And of course, you have in your Gifted program 8% vs. about 4.5% in the overall state of Florida. So, what that really says is that what you're doing, is you're really helping a lot of people move up into doing very positive things with their lives. That's really phenomenal.

So, is there anything, before I let you go, that you would like to wrap it up with in terms of a suggestion, or a point of view in your life, to help other people?

Heather Hanson: Well, I think that when I spent a lot of time by myself, unable to work and with a very limited social life, I found inspiration in reading biographies, and I learned that we all have challenges. Whether they're apparent to the people we interact with on a daily basis or they're not apparent. The more I thought about the stories in the biographies, I thought about what I was suffering through and tried to find the commonalities.

My suffering was from disability and chronic pain, whereas someone else's challenge or difficulty could be bankruptcy, or it may be a very difficult divorce. There can be a lot of different things in our lives that can challenge us. But, to try to remind ourselves to take a step back and look at the big picture and try to count our blessings and see the commonalities that we have as humans, help each other out, and try to capitalize on what you can do.

I think that's the message that I'd like to share. I'd also like to mention that if my speaking about Redlands Christian Migrant Association interested anyone, that they might want to learn more about this organization and what it does in the state of Florida, or maybe even possibly make a donation, the website is www.RCMA.net. I also mentioned my group that I started dancing with, which is Swing Time.

And I have since joined up with other swing dancing groups, and even other ballroom studios. But, the first dance I went to, Sam Mahfoud is the owner, and he is a great friend. If you happen to be in the Tampa/St. Pete area, he has a dance every Wednesday night, and that is at www.SwingTime.info. I also mentioned my good friend Cathy Nelson, who is the owner of www.DanceForeverFlorida.com, or Dance Forever, which is a ballroom studio in Clearwater.

I also mentioned a Meetup group I'm in. If you're not familiar with Meetup, it is targeted to your local area, wherever you happen to be. You want to meet up with people who are doing something you're interested in? There's a lot of these areas that other people are interested in that you can connect with through www.Meetup.com. I just happen to be part of the photography and modeling group called Tampa Modeling Photography Association TaMPA, that is run by Sean Neumayer.

Tami Patzer: Wow! Those are a bunch of really cool things. You really are living a very fascinating life, and I know because I've seen your Facebook page and you have phenomenal, for example, fun photographs.

Heather Hanson

Heather is a life-long learner, educator, swing dancer and international travel enthusiast. She is devoted to her family, friends, and helping improve the community around her. She has 16 years of experience in education; both as English as a second language teacher, as well school administration.

She has a bachelor's degree in intercultural communications from Eckerd College, a master's degree in education from Bradford University, and additional post-graduate hours from Nova Southeastern university. She currently works as a school administrator for two charter schools, RCMA Wimauma Academy and RCMA Leadership Academy. She's a data coach with Hillsborough community public, an avid swing dancer and amateur model.

Contact Heather Hanson:

Tampa Modeling Photography Association TaMPA via: http://www.Meetup.com.

Redlands Christian Migrant Association: http://www.RCMA.net

Heather's Modeling:

https://www.facebook.com/HeatherLinnModel/

Dance Forever

http://www.danceforeverflorida.com

Deco Dance Tampa Bay

http://www.decodancetampabay.com

Swing Time!

http://www.swingtime.info

The Way 2 Dance

http://www.theway2dance.com

Meet the Women Innovators

Becky Norwood

Becky Norwood is an International Bestselling Author, Speaker and Coach. She also assists her clients to publish their books. Her own book "The Woman I Love: Surviving, Healing and Thriving after a childhood of Sexual, Emotional and Physical Abuse", has laid the ground work for her coaching programs and her upcoming book interview series, the first of which will publish in late January, "We Choose to Thrive: Our Voices Rise in Unison to Spread a Message of Inspiration and Hope for Abuse Survivors.

Website: http://www.thewomanilove.com

Facebook: https://www.facebook.com/thewomanilove1/

Email: becky@thewomanIlove.com.

Debra Crosby

Debra turns entrepreneurs into sought after speakers, thought leaders and luminaries who command the stage by teaching them how to communicate in a clear, concise, confident and compelling manner. She's passionate about working with speakers who want to deliver messages, solutions and ideas that have the potential to unite us as one, global tribe.

The founder of the Present to Prosper Studio, and creator of the TED Talk Blueprint for Successful Speeches program, she brings to her practice more than 30 years of experience as a professional presenter, trainer and producer. She trains her clients to infuse multimedia and multisensory experiences into their presentations so that they can deepen the learning process for their audience.

She also helps clients weave spellbinding stories and authentic vulnerability into their talks, so they can connect with, and match the energy of their audience with warmth in a meaningful way. Bottom line: this blue haired goddess of unconditional friendliness shows you how to own the stage and be playful with your audience at the same time.

Debra has taught 1,000s of people how to successfully present themselves via TV, public speaking engagements and in Hollywood films. Her clients have presented at national conferences, booked paid speaking gigs across the US, and landed high-profile media appearances.

LinkedIn: https://www.linkedin.com/in/debra-crosby-3651958

Facebook: https://www.facebook.com/debraleecrosby

Email: debracrosby.present2prosper@gmail.com

Dr. C. Nicole Swiner

Nicole Swiner, MD. a wife, mother of two and she lives in North Carolina. She loves taking care of the family, as a whole, from the cradle to the grave. Her interests include Minority Health, Women's Health and Pediatrics. For her undergraduate education, she attended Duke University, and went to medical school at the Medical University of South Carolina in Charleston, South Carolina. She's lived in the triangle since finishing residency at the University of North Carolina and continues teaching medical students and residents as an adjunct assistant professor with the University's Family Medicine Department. While she's not treating patients at Durham Family Medicine, she's speaking in the community, writing, or spending time with her family. Her passion is making medicine plain to her patients so that all people, from all walks of life, can understand how to take better care of themselves and their family.

Website: http://www.nicoleswiner.com

Email: info@nicoleswiner.com

Dr. Heather Tucker, PhD

Dr. Heather Tucker helps amazing individuals who want to Heal the Past in order to fully Live in the Present and Dream for the Future. Her mission is to utilize all of her past, present, and future knowledge, skills, and abilities to guide others to find their happiness, health, and purpose! Dr. Tucker is happily married to her husband Winston, and loves being mommy to son Noah. Dr. Heather Tucker holds a PhD (Human-Computer Integration), M.S. Information Systems and B.S. in Computer Science. She is also a Trainer and Master Practitioner of NLP, Certified Holistic Emotional Intelligence Coach, Certified Mental and Emotional Release, Certified Master Practitioner of Hypnosis

Website: https://anotherlevelliving.com/

Email: info@anotherlevelliving.com

Donya Zimmerman

Donya Zimmerman is the principal owner of Powerful Biz Woman. She is a business consultant, mediator, author, show host and public speaker trainer! Donya received her Juris Doctorate (JD) in law from the University of Baltimore Law School. Donya has a weekly segment entitled Powerful Biz Tip of the Week on the radio show Evolutionary Woman hosted by Kahdija Ali that runs every Monday from 5:30 PM to 6:30 PM. She has created the CYA, Cover Your Assets, business training series, which airs every Wednesday and Thursday from 7:30 to 9:30 PM.

The show features guests who educate entrepreneurs on the importance of protecting their assents while in business. Donya has conducted several workshops and speaking engagements on business startups and female entrepreneurship.

Website: http://powerfulbizwoman.weebly.com/

Facebook: https://www.facebook.com/PowerfulBizWoman/

Email: dzimmerman36@gmail.com

Marcella Romoser-Scherer

Power up your wardrobe, image and inner confidence with Marcella's expertise to be the best version of you! No more confusion on what to wear or how to wear on and off the stage. Marcella has a passion to help you look and feel amazing and has powerful tools to align your inner and outer essence to convey an image and a message with your presence that is authentic and congruent with you! A message that gives you an UPSCALED and memorable first that will attract all you desire!

Marcella has over 26 years of experience in the skincare, makeup, fashion and leadership coaching industries. She will help you to identify your own unique style with determining your fashion personality, body type, face shape, most flattering hair, makeup and clothing colors and so much more. She is a national speaker, bestselling author, leadership and image coach.

Website: http://www.marcellasherer.com

Email: info@marcellasherer.com

Audrye Arbe

Audrye S. Arbe is a clairvoyant wellness consultant, mystic intuitive artist, healer, Mom, and Grammy. She counsels thousands of people worldwide born to make a difference. Audrye knows it all starts at home. This, plus source impulse, convinced Audrye to write "The Mother's Manual, a spiritual and practical guide to child rearing and motherhood", hailed as a masterpiece. It's now available on Kindle and soon to be available on PDF. What If You Are? and Life Is Miraculous, is an ABC affirmation art coloring book that's printed on 100% post-consumer, recycled paper, and it's now ready. It's great for anyone five years young and beyond and this book will transform and uplift your vibration. It's intriguing and it piques the intellect with outstanding words, plus leads to brain enhancement with its multi-perspective.

Website: http://www.audreyarbe.com

YouTube: http://www.youtube.com/AudreyArbe

Heather Hanson

Heather is a life-long learner, educator, swing dancer and international travel enthusiast. She is devoted to her family, friends, and helping improve the community around her. She has 16 years of experience in education; both as English as a second language teacher, as well school administration.

She has a bachelor's degree in intercultural communications from Eckerd College, a master's degree in education from Bradford University, and additional post-graduate hours from Nova Southeastern university. She currently works as a school administrator for two charter schools, RCMA Wimauma Academy and RCMA Leadership Academy. She's a data coach with Hillsborough community public, an avid swing dancer and amateur model.

Website: http://www.rcma.net

Email: heather@rcma.com

About Blue Ocean Authority

Tamara Patzer (TAMI)

Tamara Patzer is a No. 1 Bestselling Author, Publisher, and Video Producer at Blue Ocean Authority. She has interviewed over 300 leaders in 2017 and was featured at the Business Expert Forum at Harvard Faculty Club, NASDAQ, and Harvard Club of New York. Tamara has been instrumental in developing a unique process called "Beyond the Bestseller" which will be rolling out in 2018. Tami also won the "Author Marketing Award" during the Harvard presentation event, and the "Human Being Award" at NASDAQ. Stay tuned for her new book, "Beyond the Bestseller" releasing February 2018.

Women Innovators Radio: http://www.womeninnovatorsradio.com/.

Blue Ocean Authority: http://www.blueoceanauthority.com.

Email: media@tamarapatzer.com